INTO ACTION

*How AA members practice
the program in their daily lives*

INTO ACTION

*How AA members practice
the program in their daily lives*

AAGRAPEVINE,Inc.
New York, New York
WWW.AAGRAPEVINE.ORG

AA PREAMBLE

Alcoholics Anonymous is a fellowship of men and women
who share their experience, strength and hope
with each other that they may solve their common problem
and help others to recover from alcoholism.

The only requirement for membership is a desire to stop drinking.
There are no dues or fees for AA membership;
we are self-supporting through our own contributions.
AA is not allied with any sect, denomination, politics, organization
or institution; does not wish to engage in any controversy,
neither endorses nor opposes any causes.

Our primary purpose is to stay sober
and help other alcoholics to achieve sobriety.

©AA Grapevine, Inc.

CONTENTS

SECTION I
THE STEPS THAT GO IN ONE DIRECTION—UP

SECTION II
OUR LIFE-CHANGING LITERATURE

SECTION III
WE CALL IT SERVICE

SECTION IV
SPONSORSHIP—OUR FACE-TO-FACE FELLOWSHIP

SECTION V
THE WRITING ON THE WALL

SECTION VI
OUR MEETINGS: COMING HOME TOGETHER

SECTION VII

IT WORKS IN ALL OUR AFFAIRS

WELCOME

Into *Action* is filled with fresh, original stories illustrating the many different ways members work the "simple program for complicated people" that is Alcoholics Anonymous. Though it is known, honored, and imitated throughout the world as a Twelve Step program, the Steps are only one element in a well-rounded AA program. Lasting recovery from our "rapacious creditor" takes place within a richly varied program of action.

The Twelve Steps are carefully designed to lead us safely along a path into the sunlight of sobriety. Joining them are the Traditions, which call upon the Fellowship's history to insure AA a healthy stability and growth. Our literature inspires and guides us with the experience of the alcoholics who came before us. At the heart of AA are our meetings, held all over the world, where the Fellowship comes alive and mutual support is the keyword.

AA service activities can be as varied as our different personalities, permitting us to give back what has been so freely given us. Alcoholism is a lonely business, and one wise answer to that is our tradition of sponsorship, another example of service that results in mutual advantage. Even the slogans on our walls—"Easy Does It," "Live and Let Live" among them—are not peripheral to our sobriety, but prove themselves to be reliably portable tools to be called upon when we most need them.

The stories and letters in this book, from the pages of AA Grapevine, published since 1944, bring our program and our Fellowship to life. In the story "Unprepared," the author, deployed to Iraq, considers the AA literature he packs in his duffle bag to be his real "ammunition," protection from the deadliest enemy of all. A resistant newcomer's temporary sponsor finally gets him to a pizza parlor in "Sponsor-Temping," where he is astonished to hear the liberating laughter of sobriety for the first time.

A mother must cut our slogan "One Day at a Time" down to fifteen-minute increments when waiting for a doctor to call with her child's life-changing diagnosis in "A Mother's Nightmare." In "Welcome to Leetown," a member analyzes why her Tuesday night Step meeting warms her heart so, admitting that the welcome she receives reminds her of the hit TV series, *Cheers*.

Each of these stories illustrates the truth that, no matter what our backgrounds, our locations, our ages, our genders, our politics, our financial status, we achieve lasting sobriety by getting into action and working the dynamic, multi-faceted program of Alcoholics Anonymous.

THE STEPS THAT GO IN ONE DIRECTION—UP

And Traditions that stand the test of time

Very shortly before his death, AA co-founder Dr. Bob made an extraordinary effort to attend the First International Conference of Alcoholics Anonymous, held in Cleveland. Despite his fragile health, he made it, and offered the historic first convention this wisdom:

"Our Twelve Steps, when simmered down to the last, resolve themselves into the words love and service." *Love* and *service*, two enormous concepts that alcoholics very often rediscover in the life-giving rooms of AA.

Throughout this chapter are stories validating the fact that the Twelve Steps and Twelve Traditions, like everything else in the AA program, are meaningful only if they are incorporated into our sober lives.

As usual, our Grapevine contributors have their own unique insights on—and experiences with—the Steps and Traditions. The author of "The Birth of Spiritual Confidence" tells us how to avoid becoming "stark raving sober," so dry that we dry up. In "Willingness to Grow," we learn how to turn our character defects into assets, with the writer explaining that less guilt means more room for making amends. Here are stories by members who have successfully integrated the Twelve Steps into their lives and have found their lives transformed. After 20 years of active alcoholic unmanageability, for instance, an author's carefully nurtured professional arrogance is softened in "The Whisper of Humility."

The Traditions are to our program's sane and healthy life what the Steps are to our day-to-day personal sobriety. One example is our Twelfth Tradition, which offers us the anonymity that enables us to place principles before personalities, an essential element in working the program, given the vast diversity of our membership. Dr. Bob was fond of saying there are two ways of breaking the anonymity Tradition: The first is obvious, the second is "being so anonymous that you can't be reached by other drunks." "A Deeper Understanding" addresses that very situation, when a physician craves the anonymity that may actually threaten someone else's survival.

"When my misery became extremely painful," writes the author of "Steps to Freedom," "I called my first sponsor, a man who had worked with me years ago. When I told him how miserable I was, he got stern and said, 'We need to start working the Steps.'" Then, later in the story, the author reports, "Peace and serenity are resurfacing inside me and my fellow inmates."

If the Steps can have that effect, even behind prisons bars, how can we doubt their effectiveness in a life of blessed freedom?

———————————————————————

WILLINGNESS TO GROW
July 1985

When I was an active drinker, I couldn't see past my character defects—was controlled and blinded by them. I resented almost everyone I came in contact with on a regular basis, especially close relatives and work associates. I blamed them for my bad feelings about life and myself. I was dishonest in my thinking and full of self-pity. I was in constant fear of others and their opinions of me. I took little action and spent my life reacting to others. My anger exploded into all areas of my life. I envied those who appeared to be successful and happier than I was. Needless to say, I was very unhappy and felt I deserved to drink.

My character defects always led me back to drinking. I was unable to accept them as a part of life—I thought I was supposed to be perfect and felt guilty because I wasn't. The guilt overpowered me. Drinking helped me overlook these character defects, but they would reappear when I sobered up the next day. I would drink again, and the vicious circle continued.

But I couldn't see any of this. I couldn't understand what was wrong with me. Left to my own devices, I was self-destructive. On my own, I had no effective mental defense, against drinking or my character defects.

After sobering up through Alcoholics Anonymous and staying sober for the last nine and a half years, I am still overwhelmed by my character defects. Left to my own devices, and without the Higher Power, I would soon destroy myself.

How does one tune in to the Higher Power? The answer I have learned from AA is to recharge my spiritual battery every day—"you can't pull today's load with yesterday's horse." I recharge myself by being an active member of the Fellowship and working the Twelve Steps on a continuous basis.

In order to have a strong defense against the first drink and my character defects, I must make acts of surrender. These include working all the Steps repeatedly; going to meetings; talking honestly with fellow AAs (sponsor or close friends) on a regular basis and telling them what is going on in my life; helping other alcoholics by showing an active interest in their sobriety and well-being; and giving service to the Fellowship. All these actions help free me from selfishness in its various forms.

I can still be blinded by character defects at times, but my freedom is achieved by working the Twelve Steps, which give me sanity and certain insights into what I ought to do. I learn, or am more ready to learn, what God's will is for me.

Saying the prayers in the Third and Seventh Steps regularly, on the phone and in person with other AAs, shows a willingness to grow. Writing out a Fourth Step inventory, as suggested on page 65 of the Big Book, is concrete work on my character defects. I admit that I have them, that I am human. Rigorous honesty is the key—especially about things I wouldn't want others to know.

Swapping a Fifth Step with another AA is a major move toward freedom from selfishness. But more importantly, the Big Book says that if we skip this Step we may drink again.

I show that I am entirely ready, as Step Six suggests, by working all the Steps on a continuous basis.

Step Seven involves sincere repetition of the Seventh Step prayer, alone or with other AAs.

In Step Eight, I make a list of people or institutions I have harmed before I became an alcoholic, during my active drinking, and in sobriety. The list can be started in seconds; I simply pick up a pencil and paper and start to write. The "Twelve and Twelve" says to search our memories as far back as possible when we write the names of people we have harmed. This helps us to accept responsibility for the past, and reduces guilt for our misconduct.

I have rewritten my amends list several times because new names appeared to me. I do not believe I would have thought of these names without the previous lists. In the process of making the earlier ones, enough guilt was removed to allow me to be aware of additional amends I owed. Freedom from past conduct was achieved when I admitted I was at fault and became willing to make the amends. Like peeling the layers on an onion, I had to take action on the first list before the other names came to mind for the next.

Step Nine is a major help in healing present relationships and clearing up the wreckage of the past. By going to the people or institutions on the written list, and telling them that I am sorry for any harm or injury I caused them, I am freeing myself from the bad effects of my previous conduct. I am setting things right as much as possible and being responsible. If material or monetary amends are owed, I agree to pay what I can now and set up a payment plan for what I owe. This type of work on Step Nine has freed me from fears about the past and given me more energy to devote to present-day living—this twenty-four hours. Working the Steps is an effective way to treat my alcoholism, and the surest demonstration of my willingness to grow.

Step Ten is a daily inventory of my conduct over the past twenty-four hours, and involves sincere, honest discussions with other AAs. I work Step Eleven by saying the prayers in the Third and Seventh Steps, the Serenity Prayer, and other prayers of surrender, in the morning and evening, and during the day. Seeking God's will through meditation is an effort and takes discipline. In a quiet place, I sit on a straight-backed chair, in a comfortable position, and repeat a phrase or word such as "truth," "God is love," thoughts about present activities or the next day's events. Then I return to the phrase or word and repeat it until my mind wanders to other thoughts. I repeat this process over and over. Practicing is the key. I began with two, three, or five minutes twice a day, and as time passed I increased the amount. The benefits are many, and vary in quality and quantity. Little daily problems disappear; life is much smoother. The effort alone provides an emotional shield from a lot of the usual worries and anxieties. Try it—it works.

Step Twelve is helping others work the Steps on a continuous basis. By working with others, we become what we should be, saving our lives in the bargain. The desire to drink is removed a day at a time when we maintain our spiritual condition. All the Steps are ego reducing in nature. They help us to be more human, and for some of us, entering the human sphere has been a long journey. When we accept the human condition and our own mistakes, the give-and-take of life becomes greater. The idea that God's will is best for us looms larger, as an eternal truth to be used in daily living. The need to prove we can do it all, without anyone else's help, is drastically reduced. Sincere thoughts toward others enter our minds more often. Life is worthwhile—tough at times, but still tolerable.

Through the Steps, the Fellowship, and the Power greater than ourselves, our lives become meaningful, and we receive worthwhile answers to the question "Can you make your defects your greatest assets?" Using the Twelve Steps of AA as my life's plan in working on my defects, I am able to create assets. My willingness to grow, spurred on by others making similar efforts, gives me sobriety a day at a time, and freedom from the bondage of self. And in large measure, that's serenity.

S.M.
Joliet, Illinois

TWELVE STEPS TO A MEETING
January 1957

When first I came to AA and recognized that all my futile efforts toward sobriety were leading only to new disasters, I realized that something drastic had to be done. The Twelve Steps appeared drastic and they were offered as the directions for sobriety. Many questions were asked, some wise, some otherwise, and the answers were there ... in the literature and from those people who actually had used the Steps to gain and insure their continuing sobriety. I don't remember how many weeks or months it took for me to understand and put into practice the complete twelve suggestions, but I do know that within the limits of the honesty I then possessed, the Steps accepted and practiced were the source of my help and that I didn't then or since ever benefit by rejecting or delaying any part of them.

Maybe it's become a habit now. I'm not even sure I planned it this way, but recently I noticed that at almost every open meeting I find myself practicing the suggested Twelve Steps ... yes, during the meeting listening to the speakers and later talking to the others who came seeking help.

I don't miss a lot of the meeting, either, and I think I gain something in practicing the Twelve Steps at each meeting. I'm told, too, that practice makes perfect ... that's a horrible thought ... me becoming perfect ... but I don't think it's going to happen, so I won't worry about it.

Coming to any meeting is a renewal of my admission that with alcohol my life was in mighty bad shape, but again I felt assured that this meeting, the spirit and the people here could help me take care of me, if I continued to be willing to let that Power greater than all of us guide me. So that reaffirms the first three Steps.

Then, as I listen to that first new speaker talk a bit about his life, I am reminded of many similar things that I did and the kind of person I was and am. Yes, I'm willing to admit those facts and acknowledge them to God and recite them, too, to someone else, if in so doing it will help him or me. I am resolved again that I don't want to have any part of that old drinking me and with the help of my creator will crowd out those parts of my character which were so much a part of my drinking life. That retraces Steps Four through Seven, which I once thought an impossible task.

Frequently, too, and almost regularly, the speakers remind me of half-forgotten people I had harmed and even though I realize now I cannot make direct amends to so many of them, yet I have learned the true meaning of "Charity covers a multitude of sins"; and exercising now, as best I can, true charity and love toward all of the new neighbors I have found, I can gainfully enjoy this reviewing of Steps Eight and Nine.

A meeting at the end of a day is an ideal spot for a continuing inventory. We cannot help but compare the actions of our day with something that is said at a meeting and the spirit of our meeting together makes it easier to promptly admit it. Prayerful meditation is a natural as the speakers remind me that my old way of viewing life led only to disaster, whereas those occasions in recent years when I learned the will of my creator and followed it were precisely the times when life was really happiness. But surely I need more help and I will prayerfully search for it.

A new spiritual awakening can come at every meeting when I give up again that old total reliance on my own omnipotence and realize that I am accepting help; and when I get to see and talk to a few new people during the coffee session I might be carrying the message a little bit, too, this night.

I'm not sure yet if practice makes perfect, but I do know that practice makes it easier and that every one of the Twelve Steps can become a conscious part of our lives and cannot alone keep us sober, but truly make us want to stay sober. They have helped me find that I can get along without alcohol ... I prefer it this way.

It's a little different every time. New speakers and other meeting places help to make it so. I'm sure that practically all of us do just about the same thing consciously or otherwise. It's a good practice and it does become a delightful and fruitful habit.

This practice made with little or no effort makes one wonder if those "rugged individualists" who often claim they never "took" the Twelve Steps might not have done so many times and been practicing and utilizing these suggestions so deep down inside that they hadn't even noticed it.

ANONYMOUS
Hartsdale-Ardsley, New York

STEPS TO FREEDOM
July 2006

I'm serving a four-year sentence for burglary in a Lancaster, Ohio, prison. I've been in and out of AA for the past ten years. I stayed sober once for eighteen months, slipped, and returned for another fifteen months.

I know the freedom that comes from working the Twelve Steps of AA. But because of pride and ego—and guilt for abandoning my family—each time my life rocketed back into alcohol, drugs, and crime.

I walked away from God, AA, my seven-months-pregnant wife, and beautiful daughter. I now see the fear I had of continuing to work the Steps. I lived under bridges, in abandoned buildings, and in dangerous drug houses. Eating out of dumpsters became routine. I didn't care if I lived or died.

I weighed a hundred and forty pounds and I'm six foot one. My hair, teeth, and toenails fell out, and I had sunken eyes. I was dying from the inside out. My clothes rotted off of me. The sole of one shoe flopped when I walked. A shower was very rare.

I reached a point of spiritual death, and didn't care if I lived or died. Too proud to call AA, I stole money from my mother's purse, along with her car keys. I found a friend living the same miserable life I was, and we broke into someone's house. While we were inside, the sheriff arrived. I remember saying to myself, "Finally, it's over."

That was January 27, 2005, the day God rescued me. They hauled me to jail. I wish I could say it's been all AA since, but that's not true.

In county jail, I struggled with self-hatred. I started to pray to the God of my understanding. When the pain became too great, I called an old sponsor. He was surprised that I was still alive.

When he visited, his main message was, "We need to work on spirituality." I read my Big Book and prayed more. My health slowly returned. Finally, they shipped me to prison.

When I walked in the yard, I noticed some guys were a little cleaner cut. They seemed to have some peace and happiness about them. I knew right away they were in AA. I asked them where the meetings were and how often. I was withdrawn at my first meeting but felt the peace and serenity that I've only known in AA meetings.

After a while, I asked to chair the meeting. Of course they said yes, but something still wasn't right. When my misery became extremely painful, I called my first sponsor, a man who had worked with me years ago. When I told him how miserable I was, he got stern and said, "We need to start working the Steps."

We worked the first two Steps through the mail. I did the Third Step with a couple of guys here at the prison. After some time passed, I called him and said I wasn't doing much better and didn't care what happened to my life.

"I want you to go out into the yard, find people who go to the meetings, and tell them that you're working the Steps and they're going to work them with you," my sponsor said.

"Yeah, right," I said. "I don't think they'll stand for that. They might punch me out!"

"Try it," he said.

Much to my surprise, the first person I approached said, "That would be great." I couldn't believe it. I suggested that he read the Big Book and we'd start next time I saw him. My sponsor had me write out the First and Second Steps, I said, and suggested he do likewise. In no time at all, there were three of us working the Steps. It was great to have four of us on our knees in prison saying the Third Step Prayer.

Peace and serenity are resurfacing inside me and my fellow inmates. In meetings, I share about the freedom I feel by working with others behind bars. Some stay and some don't have the willingness.

When I told my sponsor, he asked if I was staying sober. "Yes," I said.

"That's all that matters," he said. Today, I feel at peace with myself and the God of my understanding. I struggle some days, but the struggles aren't as complicated.

I'm up for early release in July 2006. I pray that I get it. Either way, I know that if I go to meetings, pray, work with others, and read my Big Book, I have a choice to be free on the inside.

DAVE T.
Lancaster, Ohio

THE BIRTH OF SPIRITUAL CONFIDENCE
June 2005

I arrived at the doors of AA in 1983 with a problem; I just wasn't sure what the problem was. I thought I had a drinking problem. Then someone suggested that maybe my drinking problem really reflected a thinking problem. I was sure he was wrong; I just needed to get my drinking under control, then I would be all right. Still, I had to admit I had done a lot of crazy things in my past. But that was just because I was under the influence of alcohol. Right?

Someone suggested I work the Steps on the wall, and things would improve. About this time, I heard the word "program" being thrown around a lot at meetings. I was sure I knew what that meant: Just don't pick up the first drink, and go to meetings. Yet, when I checked out those troublesome Steps on the wall, I found mention of the word "alcohol" in only the first half of the First Step, and no mention of meetings whatever! I was perplexed. Still, I white-knuckled my way through the first few weeks and virtually "lived" in meetings. Things did improve—primarily because I was no longer living in fear of the law, and I now had a supportive family of fellow recovering alcoholics.

I got a sponsor who was stumbling his way through the Steps as I was; it was a little like the blind leading the blind. But we continued, nevertheless, in the right direction, feeling our way along in the dark.

After a while, I realized I had not drunk for several months. Surprisingly, I no longer even desired a drink. I must have done something right! I had refused to pick up the first drink; I had gone to many meetings in which I ran my mouth as if I knew something about recovery, and I had made a token effort at working the Steps. I could stop here, feel self-satisfied, and rest on my laurels. But something was still wrong.

I was still the same old guy. And, on the inside, I knew that I would drink again given the right set of circumstances. My decision-making was still just as erratic; my emotions, just as uncontrollable; my behavior, just as unpredictable; and my life, just as inconsistent as it had been while I was drinking. I was still crazy despite some length of sobriety.

The Big Book tells me that my Higher Power will "constantly disclose more" as I continue in recovery. At this point, what was revealed was that I still needed to be restored to sanity. In Step Two, I accepted the possibility of this miracle, but it had not yet occurred. Then, I found what I came to call the Tenth Step promises: "And we have ceased fighting anything or anyone—even alcohol. For by this time sanity will have returned." Reading on, I was promised that the problems of alcohol would, by now, have been removed. They would no longer exist for me. How is this possible? I thought. Alcohol consumption defines an alcoholic. Fish gotta swim; birds gotta fly; and alcoholics drink. That's who we are! Then, I focused on that one simple phrase, "For by this time sanity will have returned." There's the answer, I thought. The alcohol problem has been solved because its cause has been treated.

I can't recall how many times I had heard the old-timers say that "the problem is centered in the mind." Still, I was convinced that the problem was centered in the bottle. As I reviewed my past, I never remembered saying to myself, I've thought it over, and I've come to the conclusion that it would be the logical, rational, and reasonable thing for me to drink at this moment. But how many times I do recall saying, "I feel like having a drink!" Suddenly, I realized that I had not been using my mind—I had been using my emotions to make decisions that affected my life and the lives of others. That was insanity. Emotion and intuition have a role in recovery, but I had been using them in the wrong way.

So, how was I to regain sanity (assuming I had any to begin with)? As I read on, I was told that "we are not cured of alcoholism. What we really have is a daily reprieve contingent on the maintenance of our spiritual condition." I knew there was a daily component to the program, but I thought it was in just not taking a drink for today—postponing the drink. In my early days, this thought troubled me because I assumed I was being told I would have to fight the urge to drink every day for the rest of my life. But that is not the message of AA. The message was that I could have the alcohol problem removed if I maintain my spiritual condition, as outlined in the Eleventh Step, on a daily basis. Having tapped into an all-powerful source, I could be assured that I would never have to drink, nor fight the urge to drink, again—ever. What a promise! This understanding did not make me reckless and cocky; it didn't even make me self-confident. Rather, it instilled within me God-confidence.

Now, coming up on twenty-two years of sobriety, I can say that I've finally got it: "Liquor is but a symptom" and "bottles were only a symbol." And even we old-timers, with years of sobriety under our belts, can still be guilty of "working" the Steps, instead of letting the Steps work us. We can become bleeding deacons trying to manipulate and control others, rather than serving as examples of mature recovery. We can be so dry that we dry up, and become stark raving sober. In these cases, we resemble the title of an old Paul Simon song: "Still Crazy After All These Years."

DAVE C.
Springfield, Missouri

A DEEPER UNDERSTANDING
August 1981

I had always thought, as my years in AA went on, "The other fellow's anonymity is more important than mine. I don't really care anymore. I'm really glad people outside know I'm in AA."

Ah yes, but was I being equally honest with the people inside AA? I didn't ask myself that.

I had no idea how I really felt until came a day I had subconsciously feared for years—the day a man was felled by a heart attack at a banquet, during a convention held by the AA area where I live. Another member had just received a medallion honoring him as Canada's first AA—when it happened. And the banquet chairman yelled over the microphone to 1,000 assembled guests, "Is there a doctor in the house?"

I paused, irresolute. Somebody else would come forward, I thought. Yeah, that's it—they'll have a nonalcoholic doctor in attendance for a crowd this size. Nobody moved.

Then I knew I had to reveal myself inside AA, to all these congregated fellow members, as the doctor and the heart specialist I am.

I hated it. I seemed glued to my chair. But I heard a thundering command inside my head: Look, Buster, a man is dying! Move! And move I did, going first to the man, then with him into a braying ambulance, pumping his chest and blowing into his lungs over and over, until he was rolled, pink and pulsating, onto a waiting hospital stretcher.

The ambulance men gave me a ride back to the AA banquet. "Well, doc, you sure deserve a good dr____." Their eyes wandered away from my face. "Uh, a good time. Yes, doc. Have a real good time."

I crawled back into the assemblage of AAs, shaken by this self-revelation of a yearning for "anonymity" within AA, even at the risk of another's life! Surely, I thought, this must be the ultimate in egocentricity, this cold, callous "I'm okay, James—pull up the ladder" attitude.

But then I remembered the years it took me to accept the real, hurting me behind the iron MD mask—not a professional, just a terrified amateur at life, groping painfully in the blackness toward recovery from alcoholism.

I remembered all the AA meetings I'd attended as plain L_____ (never Dr. L_____), silent through indignation sessions aimed at "pill pushers" and "weird shrinks." One word about my medical training, I feared, would inhibit the thrust of the meeting, blunt the help I needed so desperately from my fellow members.

I remembered how angry and evasive I was whenever anyone homed in on my background or education. I wanted no part of that at an AA meeting.

I remembered the eighteen months a dedicated psychiatrist worked with me through Steps Four and Five until, with his incredible patience, he managed to teach me first, to recognize who I was, and second, to accept that human being. Then, I could go on with the AA program.

How little we know, thank God, of our individual destinies, the paths down which we are led so that we may be of service, in whatever capacity.

And I thought I was cunning and devious! My Higher Power outdid me when he sent me to that AA banquet, to help save a life—and to find deeper understanding of myself and the anonymity principle.

L. R.
Victoria, British Columbia

THE WHISPER OF HUMILITY
March 1955

O ne part of our great program—The Twelve Traditions—has come to mean life itself to me.

The Traditions, as written by our co-founder Bill, define for me clearly and precisely how to get well and stay well. They tell me who God is, what He does, and where He functions. They show me what spirituality is and how I may seek and find it. They clarify what anonymity means.

Perhaps most important of all, they point out the path toward humility. It is helpful that this path is not described bluntly; rather it is whispered to me in each Tradition.

Tradition One tells me that "Our common welfare should come first ..." Not second or fourth or tenth, but *first*. Why? Because "personal recovery depends upon AA unity." So, I learn that after the Twelve Steps have been digested, my group, my AA, *comes first*; not myself, you understand, but my AA group or groups. My own recovery—my most prized possession, since it means life itself—depends upon my group's unity.

I am told how to stay well in Tradition One, and to my surprise, it dawns on me that I have received the first gentle whisper which nudges me along the path of humility.

Tradition Two tells me who God is, where he is, and what he does. It says, "For our group purpose there is but one ultimate authority—a loving God as He may express Himself in our group conscience." God expresses himself in a specific location—my conscience. This is good news to me. I have wondered for over forty years where and who God was and what he did. Now I understand what was meant, long ago, by the command, "Be still, and know that I am God."

I read on in the last half of Tradition Two and I find the second gentle whisper toward humility: "Our leaders [you and I] are but trusted servants; they do not govern." I love the clarity and force of that simple word "but." As a leader I am *but* a trusted servant; I need not govern. Thank God! I have been a dubiously trusted leader who felt that he *must* govern for too long; now I may be relieved of all of that. As God may express himself in my conscience, I am his and your trusted servant, who governs only me!

Tradition Three tells me that "The only requirement for AA membership is a desire to stop drinking." To have a *desire to stop* anything is new to me. So I receive the third gentle whisper toward humility. As I hear and feel these gentle whispers I settle more and more each day to life size, and, as a Los Angeles member has said, "Life comes to be for free and for fun."

Tradition Four brings me clearly and simply into my own right. It says, "Each group should be autonomous except in matters affecting other groups or AA as a whole." You and I are autonomous. Individually and collectively, we may do as we wish, we are unrestricted—except when we step on someone else's toes or when we step on a group's toes. Thus the fourth gentle whisper toward humility says to me, "Brother, the common welfare comes first for the truly spiritually selfish reason that your own recovery depends upon its continued existence."

Tradition Five defines in clear terms my only reason for existence. There is no other for me: "Each group has but one primary purpose —to carry its message to the alcoholic who still suffers." There is my answer. I need purpose—and I have it! I must carry the message to the alcoholic who still suffers. So I say to myself, "Thank God for alcohol and for the unrecovered drunk!" And I hear a fifth gentle whisper toward humility deep within me which says, "At long last you have come to realize that service to others is all that you have to offer in this life!"

Tradition Six clarifies the spiritual side of this program. It says, "An AA group ought never endorse, finance, or lend the AA name to any related facility or outside enterprise lest problems of money, property and prestige divert us from our primary purpose." I'm glad to know this, because now I can be on guard. I have a primary spiritual aim which money, property and prestige can bust wide open and devour. I hear a sixth gentle whisper toward humility which says, "*Your* primary spiritual aim is to carry the message to the alcoholic who still suffers!" In the role of a trusted servant, I must follow the instructions of a loving authority who lives in the depths of my soul. It says, "In all reverence carry to the sick alcoholic the message that I have given you."

Tradition Seven tells me how to obtain peace of mind. It shows me how to regain my self-respect. At long last I understand the inner peace that comes from being responsible for myself, and to myself. Tradition Seven says, "Every AA group ought to be fully self-supporting, declining outside contributions." What relief that is! No longer do I need to *wait* for contributions. I am now free to *give* contributions.

Tradition Eight gives to me, a professional man, the very keynote of humility: "Alcoholics Anonymous should remain forever nonprofessional, but our service centers may employ special workers." I know the professional life; I am in it up to my very ears; I love it. But I know one other thing, too: in my life of service there is absolutely no room for professionalism. In AA I am an ordinary human being with no more skills than anyone else.

Tradition Nine astonishes me by stating, "AA, as such, ought never be organized; but we may create service boards or committees directly responsible to those they serve." You see, in the past, I have been so well organized (or so I thought) that I almost died from it! I was frightened at first to find that I needed to be in a group that wasn't organized. But in AA I am free to be myself as I find myself at the minute, and here I find another whisper toward humility: I can be on service boards or committees, and I can be a trusted servant who is directly responsible to you, my fellow AAs.

Tradition Ten pleases me very much. I read it daily with a joyful smile: "Alcoholics Anonymous has no opinion on outside issues; hence the AA name ought never be drawn into public controversy." Just think, as an AA I need never be drawn into public controversy.

I don't have to worry about being right. Never again! I don't have to fight anymore. I've had enough of controversy.

God love our good co-founder, Bill, for taking it easy on my befuddled brain. He held off giving me Tradition Eleven until I could hear and digest Tradition Ten. I read: "Our public relations policy is based on attraction rather than promotion; we need always maintain personal anonymity at the level of press, radio, and films." Never again do I have to promote a single thing—I am free to be myself. I am free to believe what I believe. I am free to say what I believe in my own way. And I hear a whisper (number eleven) deep within that says, "The way to humility is to realize that you *need* to maintain personal anonymity!" It doesn't say that I have to, or that I should, or that I must; it says I *need* to maintain anonymity, as I need the very food and water and air that keeps me alive.

And so Tradition Twelve comes into view. "Anonymity is the spiritual foundation of all our traditions, ever reminding us to place principles before personalities." I've been wondering about this anonymity business. Now I know. Anonymity means that I am only Earle. I am just a guy like you. You and I are equal. There are no class distinctions. I am not a professional man; I am just Earle. The weather way up there on the peak of "prestige and gain" was bitter cold ... down here in the world of anonymity, it is warm and balmy. I can shake hands with you and look you straight in the eye and say, "Hi, my name is Earle." I am just one guy. No more. No less. I am one of the grains of sand that goes to make up our great beach of AA. Without me as a grain of sand, without each of you as a grain of sand, there would be no AA beach. Without the beach of AA there would be no you and no me.

So I hear the last and best whisper of all. It says: "ever reminding us to place principles before personalities." I smile a deep inward smile. Day after day I come to know that our common welfare comes first, that my God is a living authority located inside of me, that I am his ungoverning, trusted servant who is dedicated to the spiritual activity of carrying the message in complete anonymity to the alcoholic who still suffers.

I smile because in my organization I am unorganized. I smile because I need not be a professional who has opinions that he must cram down your throat. I smile because I can at last be myself, and if I don't attract anyone at least I won't promote anyone.

But mainly, I smile because you—all of you in AA—have given me the opportunity to fight for your principles rather than my personality.

EARLE M.
San Francisco, California

THE THREAT OF THE TWELVE STEPS
October 1965

The other day I happened to be leafing through some old Grapevines and came on an article by Gerald Heard, "The Search for Ecstasy," in the May 1958, issue. It's only three pages long, but it manages to say a lot—to me at least. I hope the Grapevine will reprint it sometime.

I—you—may not agree with everything Heard says about alcoholism and its relationship to the over-all social malaise of our times, but I think we can take gigantic warning from his article: we ought not to settle for tepid AA, for half-measures in taking the Steps, or for too much of the stale and flat in our sober days. Not if we want to stay sober.

No, I think we have to keep looking for something better than dullness, better than average living, better than mediocre spirituality. Heard's use of that word ecstasy may bother a little: is it excessive? I think not; I think it bothers because it is the simple truth. He says, "... alcoholism (like all addictions) is not at base a search for utter sedation. It is a desire for that *ecstasis*, that 'standing out' from the landlocked lagoons of conformity, out onto the uncharted high seas where the only map is the star-set heavens."

Breathes there anywhere a sober alcoholic for whom this passage is not deeply meaningful?

Once a few years ago I sat in a bar on a New York street talking to a newspaperman who had just lost another job for drinking. He was interested in my AA story. But he was lit up like a Christmas tree, and angry, and thoroughly uninterested in any gab about regenerating him—that day. I gave up at last. (I learned later not to try to throw the heavy AA pitch to someone who is still an active and altogether pugnacious drinker, but to save it for the sobering-up hours.) I relaxed. A thought came to me. I said, "You know, H_____, I think one of the great pleasures of way-out drinking is just that feeling of being miles apart from the boobs. You're running on a different track. Different clock. Different music. Really existentialist kick. On the knife's edge of pleasure-pain, progress-disaster." And more stuff to that effect.

I saw that I had an attentive listener at last. H_____ said that that was it exactly. It was living way-out that appealed to him, disasters or no. Living like the boobs was a bore, a drag, an accursed impossibility.

I think now that this thoroughly unsuccessful Twelfth Step effort (I pray H. may be in AA somewhere by now) helped me. I've never since stopped being aware of the fact that as an alcoholic I had better not set my sights on being just like everybody else, just as ordinary, just as unleavened. As a matter of fact, I don't really know anything about being ordinary—that is, nonalcoholic—so I ought not to set up some phony idea in my mind about normal living. No, let me stick with Mr. Heard's approach for a while. His emphasis is the one for me.

If as an alcoholic I am to "stand out from the land-locked lagoons of conformity," and stay sober, how am I to do it? Join a revolutionary gang? Go beatnik? Take up yoga?

Ah, but I have an answer, Take the Twelve Steps. Dull? Have I tried it? I certainly didn't attempt much beyond the first three Steps my first couple of years in AA. My reaction to the last nine Steps was that they were put in to round out the picture; they were pious rather than practical. One hardly needed to go that far ... and so on.

But I had, along the way, a bit of perverse luck. I got into some rather heavy weather: job, health, family, everything seemed to go soberly haywire all at once. And I was moved (I see it now as a spiritual shove) to try the Fourth and Fifth Steps, inventory and confession. I didn't do a good job. I wrote some of the inventory, but not all of it. I told some of the wrongs, the pressing ones—but not all. Nonetheless, I had an exciting year of spiritual progress out of it. I was in some important way changed.

There came a slowdown, as evidently there always must. I began to think Steps Six and Seven needed more work. Interesting. Difficult. Existentialist. Knife-edge of disaster-progress. Strange new awareness of God, of self.

I saw that there could be no "lagoons of conformity" for the man who will face his character, confess it, become willing to change it, and ask God to change it.

Dynamite! Dare I set it off? Can't I just sort of let the whole thing go, and settle for modest, quiet, unexceptionable, not very spiritual, average living? After all, X can and Y can and Z can.

Are they alcoholics?

Well, no.

And do you really know anything about their spiritual life?

Well, no.

Back to me. I needed to be other. That's why I drank. I still need to be other. Having tried the toxic way of drugs and excess, let me try the "tonic" (in Heard's phrase) way of the Steps, the way of health and joy. The Steps are the specific medicine for the thing that's wrong (or right—it doesn't matter) with me: alcoholism. They are the way to be other, and sane into the bargain.

I've come this far: I know now that what is involved in taking the AA program entire, as the early AAs gave it to us, is not the prospect of turning into some sort of repulsive goody-goody. It's the threat of being truly alive, aware, and even perhaps ecstatic. I'm coming to believe that if I do not accept all of what this program offers (demands?) but, instead, walk away from it as somehow more than I bargained for, I might get drunk.

Which is to say no more than that if I do not take AA's Twelve Steps seriously and in full I cannot expect to be "on the program."

ANONYMOUS
Vermont

OUR LIFE-CHANGING LITERATURE

So much more than words on the page

A newcomers are often reminded that they might be "the only copy of the Big Book that another alcoholic will ever see." That's another way of saying that our literature is never meant to stay on the page, but is meant to come alive through us. Integrating our literature into our daily lives is only possible because the words on our pages are never merely theoretical, they're written for one reason only: to become as much a part of our dailiness as healthy food is meant to become our bodies. "A Walking Tour Through AA Literature" is as comprehensive a guide to this printed wisdom of ours as any we've seen.

Alcoholics have a built-in forgetter. Fortunately, our literature is designed to respond to this reality. Written directly from experience, it's endlessly rich and never beats around the bush. Startling as well as soothing, our literature is a resource for nothing less than sobriety, sanity, and salvation.

In "Rare and Elusive," the writer, a seeker of antiquarian editions, explains why a first edition Big Book is no longer just a collector's item to him. Taking the printed word to heart in AA is the message of "Making the Big Book Come Alive," where a new member observes a sober father patiently answering his young son's questions, while the writer remembers that his own alcoholic answers were so often given "with fists or big talk."

Our literature can be found online as well. In "Toy Box" we hear gratitude for Grapevine's Story Archive, where one member found "an insightful comparison [that] inspires me, lifts me up, and helps me meditate on the simplicity and immensity of life."

We eventually learn the explanation for one AA phenomenon: finding new insights in material we've read over and over and over. Apparently we can only take in what we're ready to hear. And since the old-timers' ideal wish for the newcomer is for "a long, slow recovery," we relish the new insights we receive from our AA literature as they come, one day—and one page—at a time.

MAKING THE BIG BOOK COME ALIVE
September 1976

I have often heard in AA meetings that the example I set may influence another. "You may be the only copy of the Big Book he has to read" is how I've heard it. That seemed somewhat nonsensical until recently, when I went to Montana for a weekend of fellowship at the state conference in Butte.

Since I still hate to stand in lines, I was sitting at a breakfast counter at the motel while the 500 or so AAs went through a breakfast buffet. Three bleary-eyed non-AAs came in for breakfast, and I overheard their conversation.

"What's that group?" said one.

"I heard it was an AA convention," was the reply.

"Oh, the automobile people."

"No, Alcoholics Anonymous—just a bunch of kooks."

I finished my meal and went into the convention hall for the Sunday morning spiritual meeting, where I heard an inspiring pitch by a kooky priest who told of his battle with booze and his triumphs after coming to AA. During the talk, I watched some people who weren't aware that I was watching, and they showed me a little of the meaning of "You may be the only copy of the Big Book he has to read."

I was moved to tears by this kooky family. I had seen them together the day before and noticed that they looked happy. (Happiness is easy for me to see, by contrast, since I've found out the destructive influence I had on my family.) They were eating breakfast together. The father's badge told me he was the alcoholic. He was about forty-five; his wife, fortyish; his daughter, about seventh-grade; the son, about fourth-grade.

After eating for a while, the son leaned over and asked his father a question. He obviously knew his father either had an answer or could find one without knocking the boy into a corner or putting him off with "That's not important" or "Can't you see I'm busy?"

The father put his arm around his son's shoulder and gave his answer, and the son looked up into his father's eyes, tilted his chin up, and smiled with an "Oh, now I see" look.

I usually answered my children's questions with fists or big talk to cover up my character defects when I didn't know—those actions that teach children to quit talking.

A while later, the daughter shared some idea of hers with the mother and father, and you could tell how much that family loved one another by the way they glowed.

Presently, the father wanted some coffee, got up and went to the hall, and returned with a fresh pitcher. On his way back, people at other tables looked up with that empty-cup expression, asking for a refill. He graciously filled cup after cup, and I was filled with a gnawing worry—he wasn't going to get any. Again, I read from his Big Book. You see, when I go for coffee, come hell or high water, my selfishness and insecurity prompt me to fill my cup first. I now understand a little better why some people drift away from me, leaving me with an empty, lonely feeling, one of the feelings I used to appease with alcohol.

After he had returned to his cup with the dregs and enjoyed them for a while, he leaned over and slyly whispered something to his wife. She leaned her head over on his shoulder for a moment, and looked at him with one of those "when the kids get to bed" smiles.

And that family just sat there and loved one another's company for the hour.

It was a beautiful chapter from their Big Book.

JIM H.
Lewiston, Idaho

UNPREPARED *(from Dear Grapevine)*
October 2004

had been sober for about a year and a half when I got deployed to Iraq. I brought my pocket-sized Big Book and pocket-sized "Twelve and Twelve" with me. In the first month, I read my Big Book three times and the "Twelve and Twelve" four times. During that time, our deployment was extended to a year. Not long after that, my group sent me some Grapevines. Just in time! I have to admit, I'd seen the Grapevine at meetings and looked through it, but I'd never actually read it. Since then, I've found out what a great tool the Grapevine is. It truly is "our meeting in print." Thanks to the Grapevine and my Higher Power, I was able to come back sober and sane.

There was plenty of booze in Iraq. In fact, I saw people drink mouthwash and cough medicine just to get the buzz going. But instead of joining them, I read my Grapevine or wrote a letter to a friend. My group kept me well supplied. I had a pretty big collection going, but I figured I shouldn't hold on to them. What if another alcoholic came along just as unprepared as I was? So I left the Grapevines at the book swap. When I noticed some of them were gone, I was the happiest guy in Iraq.

PRZEMEK K.
Fort Drum, New York

RARE AND ELUSIVE
January 2010

I had seen the book in many different places during my travels as an antiquarian book collector, in used bookstores, thrift stores, yard sales and swap meets. It seemed as though I came across it more times than other books I saw on a repeated basis. Maybe I just noticed it more because of this odd feeling that swept over me each time I saw it, and those mysterious words on its cover: *Alcoholics Anonymous*.

I remember thinking, I'll never have a use for that book. I always looked at it as something that was written for those "skid row hobos" I so often pictured in my mind, those hopeless men who lived beneath bridges and in back alleys, standing around a burning drum of fiery trash, passing a bottle, trying to keep warm and drunk.

That wasn't me. I wasn't an alcoholic. Sure, I drank on a daily basis—a bit too much most of the time—and I did have the occasional blackout, but I was no worse off than a lot of my friends. I was inured to my hangovers—they were just a part of everyday life. I was at most just a "problem" drinker, not one of "those" alcoholics, and I knew I could stop whenever I wanted. I just didn't want to stop right then.

The book piqued my interest for another reason. I collected first editions of books, and had found through my research that an early copy of the Big Book could possibly make me some real money. I knew, in my materialistic, egotistical, greed-driven world, that I would be the envy of the book-collecting world if I could just find one for a cheap price and sell it at a big profit to someone who would value such a thing.

I pulled the book from shelves, out of bags and boxes, off endless tables and dirty blankets lying on the ground for 20 years, searching for that one first edition. I had no interest in anything past that first page that showed what edition it was. I never turned past that page because I told myself I didn't need what was in it—or maybe it was just the fear that it would surely define me.

I finally gave up the search for that elusive book when I was about 51 years old. By then, I had amassed quite a collection of rare books, dealing mostly with subjects like art, architecture, psychology, magic and death. I thought a lot about death. My drinking had increased over those years, and I would often wake up from a drunk surrounded by several of these valuable books lying haphazardly around me, or on my lap. But no matter how many books like these I collected, I was still empty inside. Something was always missing. The next book, like the next drink, was just another temporary fix, and then I wanted more.

I flew to Tucson, Ariz., later that year to visit a friend who had been sober for four years. It was Thanksgiving, and she asked me one night if I wanted to go along with her to attend an AA meeting the following day. Out of curiosity, I said I would. I wanted to finally find out what AA was all about and how it had helped her stay sober for so long. I was doing my best, but was having a hard time controlling my drinking around her. She suggested to me that it might be a good idea if I didn't drink before we went to the meeting. I told her that I would give it my best shot.

We arrived at the meeting place the next morning and she introduced me to her friends. I was always so uncomfortable in situations where I was around a bunch of strangers who I knew would never understand how utterly "different and unique" I was. As the meeting progressed, I listened to the stories coming out of these peoples' mouths, and I was deeply moved. I wasn't so different and unique after all.

I stared at a big framed board with the Twelve Steps of Alcoholics Anonymous on it, particularly at Step One: "We admitted we were powerless over alcohol—that our lives had become unmanageable."

I came to a startling revelation. That was me. I was powerless over alcohol, and my life had become unmanageable.

One month later, I put the bottle down and drove to the nearest bookstore. I bought my first copy of that book I had so many times denied I needed.

Now, as I approach my first full year of sobriety and look around my house at all these "valuable" books sitting on their shelves, I know that there is only one book in my collection that has any real value to me. It is a fourth edition paperback copy of the Big Book of Alcoholics Anonymous. It is a bit beat up, written in, highlighted, and has a few dog-eared pages. But, where I thought I would only find profit from it in a materialistic way, I instead have profited from it in a new spirituality and freedom, daily using the information and suggestions contained in it as a guide for how to live a more useful, productive, sober life.

I will always remember the times I thought I would never need it, and never turned past the copyright page.

JOE H.
Tucson, Arizona

TOY BOX *(from Dear Grapevine)*
May 2007

When I was a kid, I had a toy box. When I was in college, I had a set of encyclopedias. Now I am a senior citizen in AA, and I have the Digital Archive. [Now called the Story Archive—Ed.]

The Digital Archive takes me from the days of World War II up to now. Recently, I became curious about the word "truth" in AA literature. "Truth" has appeared over 1,700 times in the Grapevine.

Then, I came across an article so fascinating that I forgot my research. "The Serenity Prayer as a Universal Equation" was published in April 2005. The author, a mathematician, sees something akin to a mathematical equation in the Serenity Prayer. The prayer expresses truths so simple and vast in so few words that it becomes a thing of beauty.

I am not a mathematician, but an insightful comparison inspires me, lifts me up, and helps me meditate on the simplicity and immensity of life.

For me, the Digital Archive feeds my soul—my spiritual life. It energizes me and gives me enthusiasm. It helps keep me sober.

ANONYMOUS
Maryland

A WALKING TOUR THROUGH AA LITERATURE
January 1993

The many miracles of Alcoholics Anonymous work at myriad levels and in infinite ways. No two alcoholics work, practice, or live the program in exactly the same way. Some achieve sobriety and a richer more rewarding life after only brief association with AA. Others become immersed in the Fellowship with many meetings, service, and repeated returns to and reviews of the Big Book. As we say—and it is true—it takes what it takes.

I fully appreciate this and in no way want to take other peoples' inventories. However, I've observed that there is one tool used less than almost any other in our bag of tools, and that is the literature of AA.

In my view, AAs seem to be largely a verbal breed of critter and our program is at its very core a verbal program, with sharing the key element and most dynamic of its many ingredients. Reading often takes a back seat to sharing and is not as essential a tool to recovery. And yet, for achieving sobriety and a fit spiritual condition, it can't be beat.

I am one of those who started reading in my early AA days, long before my last drink, because I happened to go to meetings that prominently displayed the entire array of AA pamphlets and books not in a dark corner but on the way to the coffee and cookie counter or by the main entrance. Very soon, daily reading, perhaps only ten to fifteen minutes at a time, became part of my program, which I still practice today. Usually it's an article in the Grapevine, a few selections from *As Bill Sees It,* or a piece or two from *The Best of the Grapevine,* "Box 4-5-9," or a local intergroup newsletter.

Here are the books which helped me at the start of my AA journey and which continue to be a part of my program for sober living.

Alcoholics Anonymous. Believe it or not, many AAs admit they have never read the Big Book or have given it only a once-over-lightly. For myself, I can't conceive of having obtained anything but an unhappy, white-knuckle sobriety without the Big Book to guide me in the early months. I still derive a lot out of rereading chapters two and three because I never fail to see there a grim portrait of myself. Rereading chapter four helps keep the spiritual aspect of the program in focus and reinforces my evolving perception of my Higher Power. And the stories in the back can serve as an occasional substitute for a speaker meeting because they tell what it was like, what happened, and what it's like now.

AA Comes of Age. I have heard it said that no AA can fully appreciate the Fellowship of Alcoholics Anonymous until he or she has read *AA Comes of Age.* How true! It's not a chronological history of AA, but it does chronicle and reveal the start and growth of the Fellowship in its first twenty years and how Bill W. planned the graceful transfer of power to the membership. If you like AA now, you'll love it when you've read this book.

Twelve Steps and Twelve Traditions. I was thrust without enthusiasm into a Step study meeting even before I had had my last drink. But, wow, what a key role it played in my eventual sobriety. Reading and then listening to others discuss what each Step meant to them and how they interpreted them helps a newcomer immeasurably and lights the way for a journey through the Steps. I decided to reread this book when I began this piece and was elated at the fresh perspective it provided. The Steps came alive again for me.

Living Sober. This book was recommended to me before I had stopped drinking and was attending three meetings a week. I took this slim book with me on a long trip, feeling the Big Book was too heavy and bulky for a lot of air travel. Each day I read one of the thirty-one brief sections—each a tip for not taking that first drink. Over a period of six weeks and only one AA meeting, I didn't have a drink, which was a new record for me. *Living Sober* is a must for the newcomer, especially—but not exclusively—one who's still fighting a craving. Many sponsors give their sponsees a copy at the start.

Dr. Bob and the Good Oldtimers. Probably the least read of the AA library, this is to me its most moving. It tells the story of Dr. Bob, and it describes the early years of AA in Akron and throughout the midwest. How the early program of AA was hammered out in the crucible of trial and error is a remarkable story. For example, hospitalization for "defogging" was originally required for newcomers, most of whom were low-bottom drunks. They were required to kneel and surrender aloud in the presence of another AA member. The prescribed diet for the wet newcomer was sauerkraut, tomatoes, and Karo syrup. Many AAs carried a pint of booze around to give to the detoxing newcomer. Bill W. even gave Dr. Bob a bottle of beer to steady his hands while performing surgery just after his last binge. That bottle was Dr. Bob's last drink. I had tears in my eyes when I finished this book.

As Bill Sees It. These pithy and cogent excerpts from the writings of Bill W. are excellent for short periods of reading and a quick fix for the blahs or a shaky serenity. It is indexed to help locate topics that suit your current need or mood. One meeting I know uses random selections from this book as discussion topics.

Came to Believe. When I was casting about in search of a concept of a Higher Power that I was comfortable with, this little volume of 118 brief testimonies of AAs concerning how they came to find, believe in, and use a Higher Power was extremely useful, even inspirational. This can also serve for those brief periods of daily reading and reveals an almost infinite variety of attitudes and outlooks on the concept of a Higher Power.

Pass It On. I found this one hard to put down. It's a beautifully written biography of co-founder Bill W.'s personal battles as well as his arduous role in building the Fellowship. It's a touching and balanced story of a remarkable man.

The Best of the Grapevine, Volumes I and II. Both volumes are col-
lections of articles from the Grapevine, which has been published
since June of 1944. These are excellent for brief daily reading and
for providing an ever broader understanding and appreciation of the
critical role AA plays in the life of alcoholics from around the country.

The Language of the Heart. Perhaps the least widely known of Bill
W.'s many contributions to the building of Alcoholics Anonymous
are his prolific articles for the Grapevine over twenty-five years. One
hundred and fifteen of those articles are included here. I frequently
pick up this book and read at random an article or two whose titles
strike my fancy at that moment. I use it for my brief daily reading
period and often get swept away and read several before I stop.

Daily Reflections. I had used several other daily meditation books
for several years but soon replaced one of them with this. It is the only
AA Conference-approved collection of daily meditations. It's written
by alcoholics for alcoholics. Each day's entry starts with that AA's favorite passage from AA literature followed by a few sentences about
what it means to him or her. That each entry is written by a member
of AA gives the reading more meaning than some whose authorship
is unknown and which are broader in scope than just alcoholism.

Naturally there were many times when my AA reading extended
far beyond ten or fifteen minutes daily, because I was swept up in
some of the books. In fact it was five years before I had read them all,
so they slowly became an important part of my life.

I was lucky to be attending meetings that used literature displays as
part of their Fifth Tradition policy of carrying the message to the alcoholic who still suffers. In addition, those groups' secretaries regularly
called attention to the literature display and introduced the literature
chairman for those who had questions. Later I was attending a meeting where I noticed quite brisk sales of the books and saw that the
prices of the books were displayed on the cover via a post-it note. Many
members were pleasantly surprised to notice the low price of the AA
books, compared to the general run of prices for books these days.

So that's how I became an avid reader of AA literature and how developing this habit early on contributed mightily to my sobriety. I know it has enriched my love for Alcoholics Anonymous and heightened my awareness of the miracle of the Fellowship. I suspect many AAs would likewise find their AA experience enormously enriched if they put this lesser-used tool to work.

ERNIE K.
Indian Wells, California

LET THERE BE LIGHT
May 1957

This morning it arrived just like that—I mean the Big Book in braille! The postman placed in my arms four of those six precious volumes, cautioning me to not drop them. Drop them—how could I? This for which I have waited so long! The postman has probably never seen a face like mine, but homely as this "pan" may be, I'm sure he has never seen a smile such as the one that spread over it as I stood clutching the four boxes in my arms. This old face literally beamed, and the "Thank you" I gave him must have been something out of the ordinary in his experience.

I stood there for a long moment holding those boxes in my arms, clasping them to my breast as tenderly, lovingly, gently, as a mother holds her newborn infant. Then, jolted back to reality, I placed them almost reverently in my big chair. With the hungry eagerness of a person who has reached the point of starvation I quickly opened each box, my fingers gliding over the table of contents until I found Volume Two in which Chapter Five is first.

You had spoken of this chapter so much, and I have heard a little of it—so I read Chapter Five. I mean I studied it carefully, and this took all morning. First things being first, I, with the help of God, hope next to copy this entire chapter in braille so as to be able to carry it around with me along with the "Twelve and Twelve." After that I will finish reading the Book ... the chapter, "A Vision for You," must be in volumes one or five, which are probably on the way somewhere between here and New York, and I will have them also at any moment.

As I read, question after question was answered for me. The words "must" and "honesty" appeared many times over and over again. The brevity, the simplicity, the direct approach of the entire chapter was amazing in itself. Being so complicated, and so mixed up as I am, I needed something just this simple—and so did plenty of other folks, else it would not have been written in just this way.

If there was ever a possibility of the door of heaven being opened for me it happened this morning. As my fingers glided across those pages I had a sudden experience, a contact with God that I've never had before. I know you and other helpful friends have paved the way for this, that I might be in a receptive mood.

Eight years ago it wouldn't have meant a thing, but this was just the right time, the right day, and I find I am ready. I fervently pray I shall recover. It is my decision. In Chapter Five I found the key that opened the door. Should I throw away that key the door will close.

There is hope for me if I continue each moment to turn my will and my life over to the loving God of my understanding and this morning he is nearer to me ... I feel I do understand him better.

As of this moment I repose serenely on Cloud 9, being thankful in silent meditation. I know then the grim realism of this troubled world will bring me sharply back to earth at any moment, but I pray I may make a safe happy landing when the time comes.

God in his infinite mercy and wisdom has been so good to me, ever mindful of my needs, supplying me with numerous blessings—too many to count in a day. My blindness—alcoholism—addiction—and all these physical ailments that some may speak of as crosses—they are not really crosses at all, only as I make them so. They are indeed blessings, for without them God would not enter into my heart, because I would in that case refuse to admit him.

What people here on earth see of me is but a fleeting material thing, but the soul is eternal, and it belongs to God. If I continue living I know I will make mistakes, for being human I am subject to error and weakness. But I fervently pray to live my best each moment, for a just God expects no more than my best—which he knows is all I have to offer.

Being honest with God and myself should leave me no cause for worry, no reason to fret over mistakes of the past, present or future. In this way I can enjoy the happy hours, and all the good things in life. You have reminded me at times that you have shortcomings and are not perfect, but perhaps it is the imperfection that brought you to understand me, and to set my feet on the road to recovery.

ELSIE T.
Cincinnati, Ohio

EDITOR'S NOTE: Elsie did not confine her gratitude to beautiful letters ... she went on to transcribe *Twelve Steps and Twelve Traditions* into braille.

WE CALL IT SERVICE

Though we are always on the receiving end

One of the earliest AA findings was that the biggest insurance against drinking is to work with another alcoholic. In AA there are many such ways to offer selfless service to the rest of us. Twelfth Step work is the most obvious, where our one-on-one efforts may end in someone else's life-saving sobriety. But as we'll see in "A Job that Needs Doing," "AA is about the only outfit where we can work our way from coffee-maker to committee member to delegate, and in one day go back to being coffee-maker and not lose any prestige." As is true with many of our traditions, the AA brand of service is unlike any other. If our service is performed to serve our egos, that will spell trouble, and we'll be on the way to drinking again. So it serves us to strive to be egoless, realizing that the value of the gift we receive from AA is contingent upon the gift we give back to the Fellowship.

In "Doing the AA Side-Step," a writer describes the common conditions a "side-stepping" member is vulnerable to, even with long-term sobriety, and how those conditions are cured. "I have had continuous sobriety for twenty-three years, but it has been only in the past few months that I have become interested in service work in AA. Before that, I was an AA barnacle, glued to my seat, criticizing the speakers, and griping about the coffee. Now I'm on the other side of the squawks and bleeps, and I find, to my delight, I like it," says the writer.

Another Grapevine writer echoes that happy insight in "The Most Important Job in AA": "On that night, I may have crossed the invisible line that separates the indifferent from those who are aware that well-placed chairs and tables, and coffee and cookies and literature, don't just happen."

Each of these stories tells us, in its own way, that when it comes to selfless service, the other side of the "invisible line" is a far happier place. Says the author of "Step Twelve: The Whole of AA," "My self-worth has been greatly enhanced by my involvement in service. Sharing what has been given to me is a pleasure and a privilege. By trying to carry the message of Alcoholics Anonymous, I am getting stronger all the time."

STEP TWELVE: THE WHOLE OF AA
December 2007

"Practical experience shows that nothing will so much insure immunity from drinking as intensive work with other alcoholics."

When I first read that passage in the book *Alcoholics Anonymous*, I thought, That will do for me. I have had continuous sobriety since coming into the Fellowship, so I would say that it is true. When I have been on Twelfth Step calls, I have tried to keep an open mind, being neither pessimistic nor optimistic. My powerlessness over alcohol extends beyond me and it is helpful for me to remember that.

I do not get involved in family matters, offer to counsel, or advise people. I am simply a grateful member of AA there to carry this message of hope and to share my subjective experience of alcoholism and recovery. If the alcoholic does not respond, and the family is looking for help, I suggest that they contact Al-Anon, pointing out that it is a separate organization for relatives and friends of the problem drinker. As long as I have carried the AA message to the best of my ability, then that is all I can do. While I may have been instrumental in getting someone to AA for the first time, it is not I who will get that person sober. That is a job for the Fellowship as a whole and the individual's own concept of a Higher Power. All I am able to do is give them the benefit of my experience, strength, and hope; the rest is taken on collectively. I also feel it is important to acquaint the newcomer with a variety of members and meetings. That way, they can choose their own company and their own meetings.

When doing Twelfth Step work, I believe in "horses for courses"— all of us have different abilities. When asked to get involved in any sphere of service, I think it is a good idea to consider three questions:

1) Am I willing? 2) Do I have the time? And 3) Do I have the where-withal? I heard this described some time ago as a useful guide for those thinking about getting involved.

In more recent times, I am more likely to be looking to sponsor members into service and partake in other service activities than doing direct Twelfth Step work. So, when the opportunity presents itself (and, occasionally, at other times), I like to share about the benefits of service and encourage others to get involved. After all, it is our Fellowship and it needs all the time and energy that we can usefully devote to it.

One aspect of Twelfth Step work not spoken about much is carrying the message through a third party. Obviously, this is not the same as face-to-face contact with an alcoholic seeking help, but it is an important part of carrying the message. There are many people whose professions or vocations bring them into contact with alcoholics. A well-informed non-AA can point the alcoholic to an AA contact or meeting.

To a professional, a sober AA member represents the face of the Fellowship, so it is important to select our best examples of AA to speak to non-AAs about the Fellowship. When I am engaged in such talks, I try to remember that I am responsible for the preservation of the Twelve Traditions. To this extent, I do not get involved in discussions on issues that AA has no opinion on.

My self-worth has been greatly enhanced by my involvement in service. Sharing what has been given to me is a pleasure and a privilege. By trying to carry the message of Alcoholics Anonymous, I am getting stronger all the time.

Practicing these principles in all our affairs means adopting the whole AA philosophy as a way of living. Living this program leads to spiritual growth. I believe that I have caught up on a lot of the maturity I missed out on because of my obsession with alcohol. Now that my obsession has been removed, I am able to move forward, continually seeking growth. I look upon life as an ongoing learning process that is neverending. There are many new challenges to be taken on, as well as new avenues to explore. Today, I have a zest for life that, in my wildest dreams, I did not think possible.

The whole of AA is more important than any of its constituent parts, and this is something that I am very much aware of, so when any disputes arise within the Fellowship, this principle is my guide. Putting principles before personalities, both inside and outside the Fellowship, does not always endear me to everyone, but I would rather be disliked for what I am than be liked for what I am not.

KEVIN M.
Coventry, United Kingdom

A JOB THAT NEEDS DOING
February 1969

AA is about the only outfit where we can work our way from coffee-maker to committee member to delegate, and in one day go back to being coffee-maker and not lose any prestige.

Oh, sometimes our ego gets hurt. We think, They can't do this to me! Look how hard I worked for AA. I helped organize groups. I served as secretary, chairman. I got up in the middle of the night to call on sick guys. Why, that guy who got my job was taken to his first meeting by me. In fact, I almost carried him to meetings for weeks.

Then I remembered my sponsor. It took him three months to get me to my first meeting. I wouldn't be here now if it weren't for his patience and understanding. I'm glad he didn't give up. He has passed on now, eighteen years sober. I could name dozens more that were responsible for my coming from a padded cell, near death, to a sober and happy life. Well, not so happy at first. I got my family back, and then, after three and a half years of sobriety, I had a slip and lost them again. Since then, I've been living sober for over six years. I have now been married for a year to a wonderful girl, who has been sober the same length of time; we celebrate our birthdays together each Labor Day.

Now I am a responsible member of AA. Now I am part of us. For we can do what I couldn't do alone. We can wear many different hats in AA, as a committee member, as a coffee-maker, as chairman, as GSR, or as just one more person at a meeting.

But I must always take into account my ego. No matter how often it was deflated, it bounced back to "run things" for AA. I was an activist. I couldn't seem to calm down. I felt that AA couldn't get along without me! Then, suddenly, after being Mr. AA, with lots of titles, I was back home without a label. I felt lost, so I took my inventory. I took a new look at myself: what I was like, what had happened, and what I was like now. As my wife says, "It's all right to look back, but don't stare."

So now what do I do? Step aside and do nothing? No. I know better than that. After I crawled to AA, someone showed me how to walk. Now I have a new chance to help someone else out of his "wheelchair" and into the strength of the program. I can step back and look around me. I can help pick up loose ends, not as a bleeding deacon or an elder statesman, but as a working member, sober today, ready to help.

I take a look and pick a job that hasn't got a lot of glory to it. I see the Grapevine and read it through and say that everyone should read it, for it is a window on the whole AA world. Then I remember the good job Jack H. did as Grapevine Representative for our State Committee, and recall that this is one job we in our district haven't done very well.

So now I have a label. I represent the Grapevine. I read little parts of interest from the current issue. I tell the story about the time I got drunk and my subscription ran out and my little granddaughter sent me a subscription for Christmas. (I stayed sober for four months then, maybe just through shame.)

I make suggestions for getting Grapevine subscriptions to the doctors and hospitals in our area, plus getting old copies to institutions. Someone asks me if I am working my way through college selling Grapevine subscriptions. I say, "Yes," and it's true, too. I am learning a lot in my second time of growing up. Since I lost my precious titles, the meaning of our Second Tradition has finally sunk in: "Our leaders are but trusted servants ..."

I hope that old ego of mine stays deflated. I must remember that education means going from cocksure ignorance to thoughtful uncertainty. I can't live on past laurels. It's what I am doing right now that keeps me sober and thinking straight.

Anybody miss buying his Grapevine this month? If so, be sure to see me after the meeting. We have one copy left.

W. W.
Edmonds, Washington

SERVICE *(from Dear Grapevine)*
September 1974

I am a new GSR [General Service Representative], with only about four months of service under my belt. Went to the Pacific Region Assembly, came back full of enthusiasm, but just couldn't seem to communicate any of my feelings to my group.

Now I've read the May Grapevine, and I think it points up one way that works. In the "Around AA" section, the article on a "mini-conference" by F. F., Washington, D.C., describes just the kind of thing I'd like to see get started here in the state of Washington. Our state assembly will be in October, which would allow time to see about getting a mini-conference discussed there.

But I'm woefully inexperienced in the "how to do it" department, even though I have been probing into *The AA Service Manual and Twelve Concepts for World Service,* and writing to GSO and people whom I met at the regional assembly for details on putting ideas into action. It's like being a newcomer all over again. I am retired, like to write stuff, and find that AA service has given me a new interest that occupies all my spare time—and then some!

Thanks for all the good things in the Grapevine. I couldn't conceive of being without it.

R. McC.
Tacoma, Washington

THE MOST IMPORTANT JOB IN AA
October 1976

When I was new in AA, I went to the meetings and sat in the chairs and drank the coffee and tried to make sense out of what I heard. After a while, I picked up the pamphlets and read them. Later, I bought a Big Book and began to read that. I stayed sober, and my family life and my business affairs improved, and I continued to sit in the chairs and drink the coffee. But, like a small, protected child, never once did I wonder why the chairs were always in place and why the coffee was always ready when I came into the meeting hall.

Then one night there was no coffee.

When the people came in and saw no big, shiny urn in its usual place, they stood dazed. In petulant tones, they asked each other, "Why haven't they made the coffee?" I looked around for the mysterious "they."

Finally, one of the regular members rushed in from the parking lot, ran to the kitchen, took the urn down from the shelf, and began filling it with water. "They" had arrived.

"They" turned out to be just one person—a quiet little man who had faithfully made the coffee each meeting night for more than a year. On this particular evening, his car had broken down on his way to the hall.

On that night, I may have crossed the invisible line that separates the indifferent from those who are aware that well-placed chairs and tables, and coffee and cookies and literature, don't just happen.

I did not immediately transform myself into an active, useful member of AA as the result of that one lesson. But I began to appreciate a little more the efforts of the group secretary, the chairman, the treasurer, and the members of the steering committee.

Fairly early in my sobriety, my group chose me at different times to be secretary, program chairman, and a member of the steering committee. Later, in 1967, my group elected me their general service representative (GSR). It was then that my education about AA really began, and with it a deepening love of the program and appreciation of its power.

As GSR, I was my group's link with AA as a whole, the means of conveying my group's views and needs to the General Service Conference. Through me, if I acted in a responsible manner, my group in turn learned how other groups were solving common problems, not only in my area, but all over the United States and Canada.

Among the service offices I have held are district committee member, delegate, and several functions in many service conferences in the Pacific Coast Region in which AAs from seven Western states participate. This does not make me an expert nor qualify me to speak for the Fellowship. But just as we learn about our recovery program from AAs who have experienced sobriety, so I learned about the problems of communication and service from my fellow GSRs, delegates, and other elected AA workers. I would like, through the Grapevine, to share with you some of my thoughts based on these experiences and observations.

The most important job in AA, in my opinion, is that of the GSR. This may seem strange, since there are thousands of GSRs and a rapidly decreasing number of other offices as one scans the structure chart from GSR on to district committee member, delegate, and trustee. There are, for instance, ninety-one Conference delegates (from areas of the United States and Canada) and fourteen alcoholic trustees. Why, then, don't I consider delegates or trustees more important?

The importance of the GSR to our Fellowship was beautifully summed up by a trustee from Canada at a General Service Conference a few years ago: "If we want better trustees, we need better delegates. If we want better delegates, we need better district committee members. If we want better district committee members, we need better GSRs."

Practically all our service people, including the alcoholic trustees on AA's General Service Board, come from that potentially ample pool of GSRs. Yet of our 17,819 reported groups in the United States and Canada, a large proportion do not elect GSRs. And how carelessly some groups choose their GSRs; once the groups have chosen, how little encouragement and guidance they offer.

As a new GSR, attending my first district meeting, I began to grasp, at gut level, the tremendous extent of AA. Intellectually, of course, I had known that AA was more than my home group and the few groups in the immediate vicinity. But in AA service sessions, I began to feel it emotionally, and it became real. I heard the current delegate and past delegates talk about the annual General Service Conference in New York, and they communicated to me their excitement and gratitude at being a part of this tremendous, worldwide Fellowship.

Not all the GSRs shared my excitement, however. Many were confused and bored. They did not know why they were there. Some did not even care, and dropped out—often without the formality of an honest resignation. Many groups think they have a GSR because they elected one "a while back."

I learned that some of the groups did not even ask their GSRs for reports on district or area meetings. The more eager and responsible GSRs were often brushed aside or given very little time for their reports. This kind of treatment is discouraging to the GSR. It shows respect neither for a fellow AA nor for the essential AA service structure upon which the recovery of millions of suffering alcoholics eventually depends.

During my own first few weeks as GSR, I, too, had trouble getting time for my announcements. Then I made some blackboards out of panels of Masonite, two feet by four feet. I hung them on the wall in front of the room, and wrote pertinent information on them. While members listened to the speaker, they couldn't help seeing the boards.

When the chairman called for announcements about the next meeting, I'd make some announcement about service whether it concerned a meeting or not. Eventually, group members would automatically look at me when the leader asked if there were any announcements, because they knew I'd have one.

In *The AA Service Manual,* Bill W. defines AA service as anything that helps us reach a fellow sufferer. Bill lists Twelfth Step calls, a cup of coffee, and on to AA's General Service Office and Board for national and international action, pamphlets, books, and this magazine, the Grapevine.

In St. Louis in 1955, Bill—the surviving co-founder—turned AA over to the membership. As Bill phrased it, AA had come of age.

I don't believe that we have ever fully accepted that responsibility in all these twenty-one years. The General Service Conference is the ultimate acceptance of our responsibility for the survival of AA. The quality of the delegates we send to that Conference is determined by the quality of the members we choose as GSRs.

C. B.
Santa Maria, California

GET ACTIVE!
June 1980

A story about service work must have a beginning, and we may as well begin with the job in AA that is often the start of a service life. That job is coffee-maker. Service work is a God-directed endeavor; so it is inconceivable to me that it can be anything but rewarding.

In many cases, the coffee-maker gets to the meeting long before anyone else in the group arrives and stays long after other members have gone home to lead the lives we talk about so much during meetings. The coffee-maker greets newcomers and is often a focal point for group activities. Somehow, it wouldn't seem like an AA meeting without this member or that brewing beverage. Coffee-making can be service work at its very beginning.

I will never forget the guy who made the coffee in my group. He was tall and robust and had a ruddy complexion. Except for talking at meetings and staying sober, he rarely got involved in other activities. But oh, how he did enjoy that coffeepot and the countless people it introduced him to over the years!

Frank could be very cranky. You might think he was the wrong person to expose to new people, but he was perfect. In one of those mysterious AA ways, he turned out to be a gruff lamb with newcomers. He could show them that there was this thing called a recovery program and that if it kept a zany like him sober, it could work for them, and they had best find out about it.

Many a GSR (General Service Representative), area delegate, and trustee started out in the kitchen (many of the best ones, I suspect), but Frank chose not to try for those other jobs. He wanted to work the kitchen. This way, he got to confer with serene older members, as well as offer words of encouragement to shaky new people. He did all this with a bark in his voice and a wink in his eyes and a pretty apron wrapped around his pot belly.

Service work is team effort. The minute we forget that, trouble seems to pop up all over the place. The minute service workers feel like generals or presidents of corporations, they are listening to their own egos speaking demagoguery, instead of listening to a loving God as he always expresses himself in our informed group conscience. Frank was part of the team effort in our group and in our area and in AA as a whole. He often grumbled, "I can't get too far away from this kitchen. It reminds me of what a mess I was before I got sober."

One day, a well-meaning citizen who knew where we met brought a drunken derelict to the meeting room. Only two of us were there, and Frank was getting the coffee ready. The derelict was in no shape to sit in a chair and probably could have used a hospital bed. The citizen said, "This is AA, isn't it? I've brought you a new member."

Frank's face got red, and he exploded, "Good Lord! What the hell are we gonna do with this one?"

The citizen shook when he saw Frank's anger. By this time, one of the women in the group had arrived, and she took the derelict in tow. The drunk looked at Frank and said to the woman, "He's right. Nobody can help me."

"Whaddya mean, nobody can help you?" Frank said. "You ain't so special. If they can help a mess like me, they can help anybody. Wait until I get some of this homebrew into you."

The citizen left quickly, and the new guy said to Frank, "I bet you do know what it means to not be able to stop."

The neat housewife smiled, and Frank muttered, "You bet I know."

The housewife fed him lots of Frank's coffee. Frank watched him like a mother hen. The derelict did not upset the meeting once. (If he had, Frank would have brought him into the kitchen.)

You begin to have some idea of the impact Frank had on AA if you multiply this incident by the countless number of times Frank did this. He was always helping someone new or on a slip. He also helped the older members by his regular attendance at meetings.

He was probably one of those members who would mumble that he didn't want any part of "politics" or big-shot-ism in AA. Still, he liked our area delegate and even encouraged our GSR by listening closely whenever the GSR reported on the latest area assembly. He never sabotaged the group's service needs by refusing to listen or staying away on nights when we discussed the Traditions.

Frank was interested in general service activity; he simply felt it was not for him. He was not jealous of anyone in AA. He may have been in a foul mood once in a while, but there was not one sour grape in his diet.

As a self-willed drunk, Frank had fought life and God for many years. In AA, he realized that if he got outside himself by helping his fellow alcoholic and asking nothing in return, he would not only stay sober but would enjoy life. How did he get into the kitchen? I don't know. He just did.

Frank had found his service niche, and he knew it. Everyone in AA should be that lucky. Come to think of it, we can be whenever we want to be. All ready for us and waiting to be filled, the many different types of service jobs can help anyone to enjoy Sunday afternoons—even (as Frank would say with a twinkle in his eye) a former mess like me.

E. S.
Manhattan, New York

DOING THE AA SIDE-STEP
September 1954

Too many of us skip casually through the Twelve Steps, especially the Twelfth, which obligates us to carry the message to other alcoholics. But there is still another step for some of us ... The Side-Step. We side-step the obligation when it seems too much trouble to exercise it. We forget that if someone else had not taken the Twelfth Step to reach us, we would not be in AA.

You can't do much stepping without shoes, these days, and after re-reading the above paragraph I find the shoe fits me, painfully pinching my conscience.

One night recently I was seated on one of St. Petersburg's famous green benches, waiting for a bus. A young fellow who obviously had been shopping extensively in the downtown beer stores lurched into the seat beside me. He exhaled a breath on which an acrobat could have done the giant swing.

"I'm a mess," he confided. "Have you ever been messed up like this?"

"Yes indeed," I answered politely but not too warmly, and looked hopefully for my bus.

A policeman was approaching. In virtuous St. Pete, drunks are not allowed to annoy its sober citizenry. The young man saw the cop coming, heaved to his feet, and headed for the shadows of Williams Park. The law followed and gathered him in.

My bus came and I boarded it, feeling vaguely uneasy. Why couldn't I have done something? True, the constabulary do not take kindly to interference with an arrest, however well-meaning the kibitzer might be. Some years before, in Washington, I had tried to talk police out of arresting an overtaken friend of mine, and almost landed in the wagon with him.

They have a nice, new jail in St. Pete, and it is spoken highly of by alumni of the old rat-and-roach-infested one, which was pulled down because it offended fastidious winter tourists and gave the town a bad name, causing drunks from the North to take their trade elsewhere. But I preferred my own bed at home, not caring to do any penological research work that night.

I had other excuses. No extra bedroom was available, and I didn't want my good wife to be bothered with a drunk that night and next day. I had not always been so considerate of her before joining AA.

But I didn't sleep very well that night, and in the morning I thought that perhaps I ought to go down to the police court and try to do a little Twelfth Step work. But it was a raw and foggy morning (no matter what they tell you about the Sunshine City), and I reflected that the local magistrates usually advise their customers to try AA, and if they are not habitual offenders give them only enough time in jail to dry out, suspending most of the sentence if the man promises to go to AA meetings and sober up.

So I didn't go downtown, and the young man is still on my conscience. This is written as a sort of Twelfth Step penance for my side-stepping. If it helps me, and any other side-steppers in AA, not to pass up the next opportunity, it will not be wasted effort.

J. G.
St. Petersburg, Florida

SPONSORSHIP—OUR FACE-TO-FACE FELLOWSHIP

One reason why we never have to walk alone

It's wonder enough that any of us finds ourselves in the life-saving rooms of Alcoholics Anonymous. In acknowledging that, AA wisdom has established a creative and very successful tradition, assuring us that we never have to walk the recovery path alone.

Sponsorship, like all activities requiring human relationships, can be tricky, all right. As the author of "A Sponsor Can't Be My Higher Power" puts it, "I was very willing to turn my will and my life over to the care of God, but not to another drunk, or to any other human being, for that matter." Ideal sponsorship is more than handholding, more personal than mentoring, less academic than tutoring. "Listening to Walter" describes a typically healthy sponsor-sponsee relationship. Even though Walter was never officially the writer's sponsor, all the key ingredients—support, non-judgment, mutuality—were there:

"My father has never talked to me as much as Walter did. ... Walter took time to listen to what was going on in my life. When he had experience, strength and hope to share, he shared it. When he didn't have a clue, he reminded me to turn it over to God. Over the years, there were times when I needed Walter's help and times when he needed mine."

If you don't get a sponsor, we're advised in "A Really Good Idea," "You're playing with half-measures." Faced with what seemed at the time like failure with a sponsee, a member tells us in "... And Learn" that "I have no answers, only experience. If I haven't lived it or done it, I need to send the newcomer to someone who has."

AA members often spot the hand of unseen forces in these special relationships. That possibility is certainly present in "It's for You," where a sponsor-resistant member impatiently throws his cell phone into the back seat of his car. He hears a few beeps. Then, despite not having pushed any of the buttons himself, he hears a familiar voice emerging from the phone in the back seat. "Ed? Ed, is that you?"

Guess who?

———

DOWN BUT NOT OUT
April 2009

During my early years in the program, I tried doing my part in sponsoring other men. I felt I wasn't being very successful, because all of them either went back out drinking or fired me. I was feeling defeated, and was quickly losing interest. I thought I was a failure because I wasn't getting through to these men. Didn't they understand what I was trying to do for them? Sponsoring discouraged me so much that I quit doing it for several years. I felt I should leave sponsoring to people who were better at it than I was. I was involved in other forms of service work. I went on with my life, being successful at many things that I never could accomplish when I was drinking. I didn't drink during those years, but I stayed miserable. I was sober and going to meetings, but I could not figure out what was wrong.

I have come to learn that by not sponsoring other men, I wasn't reading the Big Book, the "Twelve and Twelve" or any other AA books. Oh, I read all those books when I first came in and I really got involved in service work. However, my perceived failure at sponsorship burned me out with all of it. After years of reflection, I now realize I was just inexperienced, and could not transmit to other men what I did not have.

A few years ago, a man asked me to be his sponsor. My initial reaction was fear. I didn't feel I knew what I was doing. However, I learned early on that you don't turn down an AA request. I gave it my best shot and got right into the books to journey through the Steps. Then a second man asked me to be his sponsor. I accepted. Then a third, then a fourth, then a fifth. Working a full-time job, I was spread thin with my time. I had to try to balance time with my family. It's not easy. The best way I know how to sponsor other men is to spend a couple of hours with each of them each week. If I don't spend time with them, how are they ever going to learn from me?

A funny thing happened. By repeatedly reading the Big Book, *Twelve Steps and Twelve Traditions*, *AA Comes of Age*, *As Bill Sees It*, etc., with them, I started remembering a lot of the things I was reading. I was learning as much as the men I was sponsoring. I was re-learning the program, the Steps, the Traditions and so on. Bill W., Dr. Bob and the rest of the AA founders were very crafty in putting these books together. They kept repeating the same things over and over, but they worded it differently each time. This alcoholic needed to hear these things over and over before they sank in. It is my opinion that these founders were geniuses in creating these books that would make such an impact on so many alcoholics. Sure, times are different today. However, it is still very simple language to understand, even for today's younger generation.

By not sponsoring other men, I wasn't reading the Big Book or any other AA books.

I learned about the history of AA all over again. I learned that the beginnings of this program were divinely inspired by God. There is no denying our history. The history books tell the story that several people from different religions helped the founders of AA get this program off the ground. I also learned that Bill W. had a similarly bad record as I had in the beginning, when he tried helping other alcoholics prior to meeting Dr. Bob. The difference was that he didn't give up, as I had. He hung in there, and look what he has done for millions of alcoholics throughout the world. Bill had learned, as I finally learned, that it was not his fault if the alcoholic he was trying to help went back out drinking. He, Dr. Bob, and the rest of the founders continue to teach me every day how to be a better sponsor.

All I have to offer the people I sponsor is what the founders of AA passed down to me through the books they wrote. That is the AA program. I also have my personal experiences to share with them, and how I apply the AA program to every aspect of my life. Once

I try to teach them things I make up in my head, I'm inventing my own modified program. I'm also diluting this gift I was given that has saved my life. What right do I have destroying a sponsee's life by teaching him a bunch of garbage I made up, instead of this gift that was so freely given to me? As long as I stick to the information in the books that the AA founders passed down to me, they are going to learn, and I'm going to learn.

Am I still miserable, as I was through those years that I was not sponsoring anyone, or doing much of anything else? No, I'm just grateful that I didn't go back out drinking. I realize today how close I came, and I don't recommend doing what I did to anyone. I have a lot of peace and serenity today. I'm happy with both my self-esteem and self-worth. I'm confident in who I am. I have never been happier in my entire life. I am totally convinced that the reason I feel the way I do is that the AA Steps and Traditions are a big part of my life on a daily basis and I'm very involved in service work today. All this involvement in the program is the key to happiness, and the other things I have described above. I wish success in sobriety to all alcoholics. It will turn your life around if you just give this program a chance.

JERRY L.
Phoenix, Arizona

LISTENING TO WALTER
August 2010

EDITOR'S NOTE: Though Walter was never officially the writer's sponsor, her tribute to him is a perfect illustration of the principles and practice of great sponsorship, where healing and support invariably work both ways.

I met my friend Walter one Christmas Day when I took my children to a nursing home to do service work. They walked around with me, passing out decks of playing cards, pairs of socks and sugar-free candies. We passed a table where a man in a wheelchair was talking to a friend. I heard him say something about "the Big Book" and "the Steps," so I stopped and asked if he was a friend of Bill W. He was. I introduced myself and he told me he'd been sober for about 25 years. He couldn't get to meetings much anymore because he was in this home, stuck in a wheelchair. It was hard for him to get around, so I offered to bring a meeting to him.

Once a month, I'd visit Walter in the nursing home for a Big Book study. Sometimes a friend or two would join us, but mostly it was just Walter and I talking program. If I couldn't go, one of my sponsees went in my place. I had been sober for a while by then, but I learned a lot about recovery listening to Walter's stories. It turned out, by the way, that the conversation I'd overheard on Christmas Day was the first time he'd spoken about recovery to anyone at that nursing home.

A few years later, I moved away and Walter changed homes. We lost touch for six months, but he found me again right around Christmas. My husband and I had just separated, my sponsor was out of the country, and I was having a very hard time. I'd put the kids in bed around nine, then wash dishes and straighten the house. At ten, when my work was done, the fears would rush in. That was when the phone would ring. It would be Walter, calling to say hi. I don't know how he knew exactly when to call, but that voice on the phone got me out of my fears and back into grace. We'd talk about the weather. He'd tell stories about his childhood in the South. He told me about the jobs he'd held. And we talked about recovery.

Walter was almost 70 when I met him and he still referred to his parents as "Mama and Daddy." My father has never talked to me as much as Walter did. Even when we have the opportunity, he's too busy, too distracted. Walter took time to listen to what was going on in my life. When he had experience, strength and hope to share, he shared it. When he didn't have a clue, he reminded me to turn it over to God.

Over the years, there were times when I needed Walter's help and times when he needed mine. At one point, he moved into a nursing home nearby. Helping him move in, getting his furniture there and picking up his groceries got me through the first summer my children spent away from me. That summer, I even found a way to get him to a real AA meeting at my home group and we went out to breakfast with some of my friends afterward. He'd thank me for helping him. I don't think he really knew how much he helped me.

Walter died a year ago, and I had the privilege of attending a memorial service for him and meeting the friends and family members I'd heard so much about through his stories. Among his belongings, we found all of his AA coins rolled up in paper like a stack of silver dollars. Everybody took one to remember him by. I've got his 15-year coin on my keychain, where it's been since my anniversary last spring. I think of him every time I see it.

A.D.
Texas

SPONSOR-TEMPING *(from Dear Grapevine)*
March 2007

I got "kidnapped" in December of 1995. After my third AA meeting, Henry R. announced to the group—and to me—that he was going to be my temporary sponsor. The next thing I knew, I was crushed into the back seat of a Lincoln, and off we drove to eat pizza.

I was listening to the laughter of Jack, Henry, Petey, Ruby, and others who met us at the pizza place. They seemed too happy. I checked to see if they were wearing belts and shoelaces—I had just gotten out of the funny farm and I knew that only non-clients had belts and shoelaces. But these men had both, as well as the kind of life I wanted.

I worried about paying for my only meal that day. But, much to the delight of me and my empty wallet, Henry paid. He said it was his pleasure.

Maybe I would have gotten sober without a temporary sponsor—I don't want to think about the alternative. Maybe some don't count temporary sponsors, but I might not have lived without their help.

R.W.G.

IT'S FOR YOU *(from Dear Grapevine)*
May 2004

I'm pretty typical in having a thirty-pound phone with electrified buttons that keeps me from calling my sponsor as often as I should. I was out of town on business, and I went into the local post office to mail a small package. I had my cellular phone in my jacket pocket.

When I returned, I heard a few beeps come from my jacket. I reached into my pocket, grabbed the phone, and tossed it onto the seat next to me. Within a few seconds, I heard this voice that sounded a lot like my sponsor, "Ed, Ed, is that you?" The voice was coming from the phone. Somehow (Higher Power) the correct sequence of buttons had been pushed to get my sponsor on the phone. We had a great laugh about it and chatted for a few minutes. Is that cool, or what?!

ED K.
Groton, Connecticut

...AND LEARN
November 1996

I am always quick to acknowledge the contributions my sponsors have made to my sobriety, but I often forget the growth I've attained from the ladies I sponsor.

I became a sponsor for the first time when I was eleven months sober. I'd never read the pamphlet on sponsorship so when Tina would call with overwhelming newcomer problems, I'd pick her up, bring her to my house, tuck her into bed with a stuffed animal, and say, "We just won't drink tonight and tomorrow everything will get better." Somehow it always did and eight years later Tina is a sober mother and almost finished with nursing school. I wasn't so lucky with Beverly. After release from a mental hospital, she checked into a hotel with a bottle of pills and a quart of vodka. I learned that I have no answers, only experience. If I haven't lived it or done it, I need to send the newcomer to someone who has.

Jackie taught me to live and let live. She gave me the courage to leave my grown children so we all might make our own decisions and lead our own lives. Five years later, we are all doing well and one daughter has joined Al-Anon.

I'd never been to a prom so being Kim's bridesmaid and wearing a formal filled that void. Later I was allowed to witness the miracle of her daughter's birth. Phyllis taught me about kindness, and Sheila taught me to be a friend. Shirley taught me to never give up, Rose taught forgiveness, and Vickie taught trust.

I came to AA looking for a way to drink like a lady. What I found was hope and self-respect, unconditional love mixed with honesty, tolerance, and understanding. By working with others I'm allowed to witness the miracle of sobriety and observe the twinkling eyes as others learn to speak the language of the heart. Like me they came to scoff and stayed to pray. I thank God for lessons learned and pray that I'll never be too old or too rigid to learn from everyone in the Fellowship of Alcoholics Anonymous.

EILEEN K.
Orange, California

A REALLY GOOD IDEA *(from Dear Grapevine)*
November 2003

I agree with the author of "No Absolutes in AA," (Aug. 2003) that "setting down a rigid command" could tend to alienate newcomers. But I think it is just as dangerous to say at the group level, "I've just celebrated eight years of sobriety, and I've never had a sponsor."

There are many "musts" in the first 164 pages of the Big Book. One happens to be about sponsorship: "He suddenly realized that in order to save himself he must carry his message to another alcoholic."

I came into AA an absolutely broken and dispirited man. During my last drunk, I hurt my wife, and she very wisely left me. After detoxing on the floor of my apartment for a few days, I crawled into AA. Through the fog of my early days, I used to hear "Half measures availed us nothing," and every time I heard it, I knew they were talking about me. I had tried to quit drinking for seven years before I came to AA. The message where I got sober was clear: If you didn't get a sponsor, you were playing with half measures.

After eight months of working with my sponsor, going to two

meetings a day, my wife (who works a great Al-Anon program) called and said she might like to see me: an AA miracle. We got back together, and two years ago we gave birth to our first Al-Atot. (Technically she did the birthing, but I was there—sober and grateful.)

It's true that the only requirement for membership in AA is a desire to stop drinking. But if you absolutely want a better life, well, hmm ... How's this? Working the Steps with a sponsor is a really good idea.

CHRIS R.
Spring City, Utah

A SPONSOR CAN'T BE MY HIGHER POWER
May 1972

When I first came to Alcoholics Anonymous, a beaten and whipped specimen of a human being, I witnessed a great many things that absolutely appalled me. But, considering the shape I was in and having already rejected AA on three or four occasions, I thought it best to keep my pearls of wisdom to myself—in simpler language, to sit down and shut up.

Fortunately, I stayed around long enough to find out that most of those things that I detested had nothing to do with the program of AA. It was also fortunate for me that I stayed to see some of my notions change with my own growth and continued sobriety.

But after four years of beautiful living through the program of AA, I still find myself concerned over one or two of the things that appalled me in the beginning. I have waited to express my feelings, thinking that they, like many others, would change with my continued growth. But there is one subject on which my feelings have not changed at all, and that is sponsorship.

When I was a newcomer, the question "Who is your sponsor?" was thrown at me with such increasing frequency that I began to feel guilty for not having one. In fact, I heard at a discussion meeting in those early days that without a sponsor a slip was inevitable.

Not wanting to fall to the futility of alcohol again, I began my search for my sponsor. What I saw was astounding!

As I listened to the many speakers at the podium who had been entrusted with sponsorship, I wondered why some of them referred to those who were seeking their help as their "babies." Had they taken control of the newcomers' lives? Don't the Traditions state that "there is but one ultimate authority—a loving God as He may express Himself in our group conscience" and that "Our leaders are but trusted servants—they do not govern"? What then was this control and possessiveness which prompted a "my baby" or "one of my babies" attitude toward a newcomer?

I was very willing to turn my will and my life over to the care of God, but not to another drunk, or to any other human being, for that matter. And yet I didn't want to get drunk and they were saying I would if I didn't get a sponsor. It was terribly confusing. For the sake of sanity and sobriety, I began working on the Twelve Steps, hoping the answer would come.

As I watched and listened, I became more discouraged with the idea of sponsorship. I have seen sponsorship cliques that are like exclusive clubs within AA. In these cliques, the so-called babies are told what meetings they are to attend, whom they are to go to the meeting with, whom they may or may not date, and what to do with their weekends. I know of one case where the "babies" do all the housework and yard work for their sponsor every weekend, at his command.

I was about six months sober when I finished my Fourth Step, and I needed someone to take my Fifth Step with. I asked a man I had been rather friendly with whether he would be my sponsor. He agreed. I immediately took my Fifth Step with him. He was kind and considerate and laughed a lot at my confessions. He has been a dear friend and has given a lot of wisdom and understanding to our friendship. But his efforts have not been any more valuable than the sharing I've done with some other close friends in AA.

It became necessary for me to find another sponsor, with whom I would feel closer identification. I did, and he is a beautiful man. He has a marriage of the nature that I hope some day to have. He has a humility that I hope to attain some day. He is an inspiration to his fellowman, as I hope to be some day. But he does not tell me what to do with my life. Our relationship has been one of sharing the bad and the good—our "experience, strength and hope." When I asked him to be my sponsor, I might as well have asked him to be my friend. That is what he has been.

Sponsorship is a gift! It is not a favor we extend to another human being. It is as important to our own sobriety as it is to the sobriety of those who receive it. "Alcoholics Anonymous is a fellowship of men and women who share their experience, strength and hope with each other that they may solve their common problem and help others to recover from alcoholism."

Besides giving each of us the miraculous gift of sobriety, God has also given each of us the gift of our own individuality. They are both priceless gifts. Through our individuality and growth in AA, we come to find in what way we can best serve our fellow alcoholic and what purpose we are to serve here on earth. There is only one way I know to accomplish these ends—by leaving my life and my will in the hands of God. Just as there was no human power that could have relieved my alcoholism, neither is there a human power that can run my life. We are God's babies. We belong to no one and no one belongs to us. We are here to serve, to share, to love, and to fulfill God's will for us to the best of our ability.

DEAN S.
Santa Monica, California

THE WRITING ON THE WALL

Our sober slogans lead to saner attitudes

In a Grapevine editorial written in the relatively early days of AA, titled "Using the Slogans," we are reminded that the suggestions we see on our walls at meetings are "simple but powerful remedies ... AA tranquilizers." Years later the author of the story "Living the Slogans" described them as "cute little banners ... that can change my day." These words of wisdom of ours are invariably brief messages, and that's a good thing, since when we first enter AA the simplest possible suggestions are all we can handle. We'll ask an old-timer, "Why is the 'Think' sign upside down?" The answer might be just what we need to hear to set us right at that particular foggy moment: "It means don't think. Not right now. Just don't drink, go to meetings, and take suggestions."

"Easy Does It," we're told in the story "Has Advanced," means "Don't fret and worry and stew and struggle," which is, by the way, an excellent countdown of favorite alcoholic attitudes. We know the slogans are working when newcomers report that they're getting sober one phrase at a time.

"Keep It Simple" is a more profound suggestion than it at first appears. Those were co-founder Dr. Bob's last words, said on his deathbed. They were wisely spoken, since alcoholics can complicate just about anything, we are fond of reminding ourselves. It's a gift to be simple, indeed, when chaos once had the run of your life and your thinking.

Some of our key slogans, such as "A Grateful Heart Will Never Drink," haven't made it to the bumper sticker stage, but they are emblazoned on our daily list of intentions. True humility carries similar weight in our program, a member writes in "Most Humble," pointing out the folly of displaying showy pride, even pride in our amount of sober time.

They are our slogans, and we love them. More important, they will ease our way into sobriety, if we live them.

STICK WITH THE BASICS
March 1978

One of the lines I heard when I first came into AA was "There are no musts in AA, but there are a good many 'you'd betters.'" I've been in the program for a number of years now, and I find a refresher course in these essentials is always helpful. So I got together with some AA friends, and we made the following list of what seem to us the "you'd betters" or basics of AA for anyone who wants to achieve sobriety and keep it.

• Recognize your problem, and know that you can't stay sober by willpower alone.

• Get to as many meetings as you can. (Meetings are insurance against drinking, so the more meetings we attend, the greater our insurance. It is also at the meetings that we share our "experience, strength, and hope" with each other.)

• If you are a newcomer, get yourself a sponsor—someone who seems to make sense to you, has quality sobriety, as well as quantity, and is of the same sex.

• Live twenty-four hours at a time. (Concentrate on living a full life *today*. There isn't a thing we can do about yesterday, and tomorrow never comes.)

• Surrender your will and your life to a Higher Power. (In other words, get out of the driver's seat.)

• Be willing to listen and learn.

• Follow the Twelve Steps, which are the cornerstone of the program.

• Practice the Serenity Prayer.

• Use the slogans: "First Things First," "But for the Grace of God," "Easy Does It," "Live and Let Live," and "Think."

- Abide by the Twelve Traditions.
- Realize that it is the first drink that triggers off more drinking.
- If you are tempted to take that first drink, either call another member or call on God (he's always home) or put off taking the drink until tomorrow (which, if you are living twenty-four hours at a time, never comes).
- Try to live honestly in every aspect of your life. If you have a slip, confess it publicly to your group.
- Keep the program simple. (Don't analyze. Utilize.)
- Avoid excess of any kind—that is, don't get too hungry, too angry, too lonely, too tired, too anything.
- Carry your share of the work of the group.
- Avoid resentments and self-pity—two dangerous attitudes that we alcoholics cannot afford to have.
- When you can't cope, turn your problems over to a Higher Power rather than turning to the bottle.
- Remember that you can't keep your sobriety unless you give it away. (Helping others is the foundation stone of recovery.)

AA FRIENDS
Claremont, California

HAS ADVANCED
July 1948

One of the most useful of the sayings that have been adopted in AA is that which advises, "Easy Does It." So universally workable is this good advice that it qualifies as the expression of one of the fundamental steps in personal rehabilitation.

If this particular saying is applied sincerely and intelligently, it will greatly ease the path of the newcomer in AA, avert "slips" and further the development of a mature life both inside and outside AA.

Axioms are only words in themselves, of course, and the phraseology has become trite in many cases. Pseudo-intellectuals are especially scornful of old sayings, and even less snobbish observers may overlook the worth to be found in the meaning behind the words.

For example, "Easy Does It," means—relax! Don't fret and worry and stew and struggle! Take it easy! Relax!

Everyone who has an intimate knowledge of the alcoholic will agree that one of the first things he needs to do is to relax, not only in the early stages of AA but forever after and a day. "Easy Does It" applies no matter how long one has been in AA and, in fact, it is essential to continued progress in AA and to a return to more normal living outside.

Physical relaxation has long been identified as a characteristic of great athletes. The DiMaggios and the Williams have an easy swing that belies yet accounts for much of the power of their bats. The fastest of swimmers relax with each stroke. In football, the relaxed player is less prone to fumbles and injuries. The great runners have a relaxed stride even when they are driving the hardest.

Relaxation frees the intellectual, the emotional and even the spiritual functioning of the personality no less than it loosens the muscles of the body.

"Easy Does It" for the newcomer during those first early days of confusion, fear and doubt. If, instead of worrying and "tensing up" because he does not grasp the whole AA program in the first sitting—if he will relax, he will find that the emotional understanding as well as the intellectual understanding of the AA philosophy will come along much more readily.

Fortunately, this is a saying that can be tested easily. It does not have to be accepted on faith alone. Anyone can find out for himself whether it works simply by trying it himself.

Suppose a problem has arisen. Suppose it is the old urge to reach for the bottle. Or suppose the problem is one of those by-products of alcoholism that continue to come up long after the urge to drink has gone. The reaction of the alcoholic, and of more than a few nonalcoholics, is to fight the problem, to worry about it, to get into a stew. The tension begins to mount. Emotion runs wild. Self-control is slipping rapidly.

That's the usual sequence. It can be broken if in the midst of it the victim sits way back, physically and mentally, and relaxes. First he must relax his muscles, because that's the easiest to do. Then he must relax his mind, by directing his thoughts to pleasant subjects, to a reminder that others have succeeded and so can he, to mental pictures of peace and success. If he will but direct his mind away from the problem, he will find a new source of strength rising up within him.

At least that is the way it has worked and still works for others. The individual who has learned how to relax has already advanced a long way toward happiness and success.

Relax and enjoy AA. Relax and enjoy life.

"Easy Does It." If you don't believe it, try it.

J.M.D.
Nashville, Tennessee

A MOTHER'S NIGHTMARE
November 2010

In February of 2009, when my son was 9 months old, he woke up with a droopy eyelid. I noticed that his left eyelid was practically closed. I tried to stay calm, but my mind goes to terrible places when I'm scared. I had to wait almost two hours until the doctor's office opened, and by the time it did I was a nervous wreck. I did spend some of that time praying, but only between the Internet searches for "droopy eye."

The doctor looked at my son and said it would probably go away on its own. I don't do well with "probably." The doctor told me to wait two weeks. If it didn't go away, I should call an ophthalmologist. I called one for an appointment as soon as we got home.

There was more waiting. Meanwhile, Caden's eye was drooping on and off and my husband had to institute an Internet search ban in our house so I would stop trying to diagnose our son. We went to the appointment with the ophthalmologist and she gave my son a complete eye exam. Everything looked fine, but she suggested we see a neurologist. "It's probably nothing," she said "but it may be something very serious and you need to get it checked out." Another "probably." Not good, and there was more waiting and more intermittent eye drooping.

The day finally came for the neurologist appointment. I held my chubby little 10-month-old while the doctor poked and prodded at him. Then she told me what she wanted to do. "I'd like to do an MRI of his brain so we can rule out a brain tumor." I absolutely shut down. My worst fear—that one of my children could be devastatingly ill—was right in front of me. I had no choice but to walk through it, but I didn't know if I could.

I was running on autopilot. I still didn't really believe this was happening. When we got in the car to drive home, I put on the saddest country music I could find and let the self-pity wash over me. I cried for my baby and what he was going to have to go through, and I cried for myself. I didn't think I could do this without drinking. I didn't want to feel these feelings, and the best way I know how to not feel is to drink.

It only took a couple minutes of this way of thinking before I called my best friend Jenny, another recovering alcoholic. "They think Caden might have a brain tumor," I told her, "and I want to drink."

"I know you do," she said. "But you can't."

I told her I knew that. It wasn't an option anymore. "Well then, I want to sit in the corner, rock, and pull out my eyelashes," I told her. It was the only other thing I could think of to do.

"You can't do that either," she told me. "You have two little kids and you need to take care of both of them. You are going to walk through this sober." I didn't really believe that I could, but I believed that she believed I could, and for that moment, that was enough.

We had three days until the MRI. I was trying to figure out how I was going to get out of bed the next morning, when I realized I didn't have to. I didn't have to figure out anything. All I had to do was make a decision to turn this over to my Higher Power, to ask for the ability to live in this moment, right now, as it was happening.

Soon enough, these moments would take me to the MRI, and I'd deal with that then. I had no idea what to do next, so I asked God to help me do the next right thing.

Then my kids told me they were hungry. OK, I thought. I can do this.

Feed the kids. A while later, I found myself worrying again, thinking about the test. Again I asked God for guidance. The doorbell rang and when I opened it, the dog ran out. OK, I thought. I can do this. Go find the dog. And that's how it went for the next three days. Moment by moment, I asked for and received God's help. I was so afraid that the only possible way to make it was to stay in that exact moment.

My son ended up being OK—no brain tumor, just a sometimes droopy eye that he eventually grew out of. I am grateful that I was able to walk through it sober and with a small amount of grace and dignity. I did it by going back to the basics—living one small moment at a time and trusting that God was with us. Not that God was necessarily going to make everything OK—my version of OK, where everyone is healthy and there is no bad news—but that no matter what, God would help us walk through our lives moment by moment.

JENNIFER S.
Huntley, Illinois

THINKING IT THROUGH
October 1982

The discussion meeting had actually ended. The last member present had spoken. But throughout the room, hands were shooting up to be recognized.

"Can I say something?"

"Let me comment on that."

"I want to add something, too."

The discussion topic had been AA's slogans—which ones we like best and use the most. The last speaker had mentioned "Think, Think, Think." That was the slogan, he said, that he disliked the most. Thinking was what had fueled his drinking. He wished we could scratch that slogan. The room cheered, and individuals clamored to concur.

It's true that before I entered Alcoholics Anonymous, about all I did was think, think, think. I was so busy thinking about what had happened at work earlier that I never noticed how much gin I was drinking. I was so busy planning what I would say to some son of a gun tomorrow that I neglected to plan supper.

My thoughts were sick, and I regarded myself as a victim of those thoughts. I never took responsibility for them. I guess it never occurred to me I could have thoughts that weren't wildly anxious or desperately depressed.

When I entered AA, the quality of my thinking would clearly have to change if I was to stay away from that gin. So my sponsor explained our slogan to me. "Think through that drink before you pick it up," she said. "Remember the events that turned your last drink into your last drunk? Think through the horror of your actions, the physical pain of the morning after, the remorse you felt, the disgust in the eyes of your husband.

"Think," she said, "think, think before you make that angry comment or mail that bitter letter. How important is it? Perhaps we have no control over what thoughts occur to us," she explained, "but we must take responsibility for the thoughts we allow to remain. Especially, choose thoughts of gratitude over thoughts of discontent. Think how much you've gained before you risk what you have."

Lots of times, newcomers don't interpret our slogans accurately. We patiently explained "Easy Does It" to the newcomer who is anxious to assume it means "Don't bother going to work."

And when we do explain it, we give the newcomer hope. With practice, we explain, we gain a new perspective on the things we do that brings new peace of mind. Life will not always be as stressful as it has been.

Similarly, we must explain "Think, Think, Think" to give the newcomer hope. As we recover in AA, the part of us that was the sickest—our thoughts—will also recover. Allied with God, the newcomer learns, our thoughts become more healthy and more trustworthy.

H. G.
Dallas, Texas

USING THE SLOGANS *(Editorial)*
November 1958

I was wondering what you thought when you came to your first AA meeting and saw the slogans displayed, as we have them here and at other AA meeting places in the area. Our little signs are—Easy Does It, First Things First, Live and Let Live, and But For The Grace Of God. I know groups elsewhere have other thought-provoking slogans and I'm sure they all are helpful. I don't recall my original impression, but I'm quite sure I could not figure what these sayings could possibly have to do with me or my newfound desire to stay sober.

The slogans are simple things, we have heard these phrases many times before. Probably their wisdom has served many generations. Even though they may be ages old, it seems as though they were designed especially for us. They can help when we fit them to our everyday needs.

Often I think of the slogans as reminders and, in our present day language, consider them as "tranquilizers"—which are mighty handy to have around. Because we hear and see them frequently, they have become very familiar and can remind us, in moments of stress or indecision, just what is best for us. Since I, personally, do not believe in the use of the medical tranquilizers, I have found these AA tranquilizers to be mighty efficient when facing self-pity, resentment or any of the other woes that are dangerous to the alcoholic.

Maybe you, too, can get some assistance from them, as have so many others. Easy Does It is the one that probably first attracts our attention. Though this reminder suggests something absolutely contrary to our past performance, still these words have their appeal and maybe even a touch of humor when we learn to smile at ourselves as we slow down.

All of us have our many problems and troubles. We would like to believe we could sober up quickly and take care of all of them immediately, but it doesn't often work that way. However, if we can reach out for this thought—Easy Does It—when we seem to panic at an avalanche of troubles, fears and doubts, we might get to know, habitually, that the best way to handle all things is "Easy." It can also be a cautious check on the over-zealousness of the newcomer, who might rush to do too much in too short a period of time.

This, of course, does not suggest that we put everything off until tomorrow, for there are many worthwhile things we can do today. The reminder is, do it but Easy Does It. You'll find yourself enjoying the use of this tranquilizer, taken in moderation and at the proper time.

Then there is another—First Things First. That's a real gem. If only it were possible, in our confusion, to keep this foremost in our thoughts, we would have gone a long way toward successfully coping with most of our troubles. Quite naturally we in AA contend that the first thing to avoid is the first drink; then there is a good chance that everything else can be cared for later. Unless the first drink is avoided, not much else matters. We emphasize that as being of first importance always. However, we will encounter other situations where a mental flash of this reminder can enable us to set our thinking in order, so that we can decide what should be our first consideration and what is less important. Truly, these AA tranquilizers do not solve our problems, but they can calm us down, remind us of a better way to proceed, and perhaps even put us in a mood to make better decisions.

The reminder of Live and Let Live can come in very handy many times. Some may consider it as a plea for tolerance—letting the other fellow live his life with his faults so that he won't criticize our imperfections. Others have found this a good suggestion to preserve harmony within the family or group. It can remind us to pause and reflect a moment whenever we feel inclined to gossip, criticize or envy others with whom we must live.

Others like to think of it in a more positive fashion. When disturbed by the actions or opinions of others, they are reminded that they were put on this earth to live their own lives. The emphasis is on living, based on truths, as they understand them—living with as much honesty as they can command. Perhaps this suggests that when we live our own lives we will have little inclination to find fault with the efforts of others. Live and let live.

But for the Grace of God is another appropriate reminder. This, too, is subject to different interpretations and a variety of uses. At one time this phrase came to mind whenever I heard of someone whose history of alcoholism involved greater hardships and seemingly more misery than mine. I was happy that I was more fortunate than they.

I no longer make such comparisons. Rather I use this reminder as a prayer of thankfulness for the many favors and bountiful help I receive each day. I remember that whatever sobriety and little capability I may have today is the result of the mercy and kindness of an ever-loving God. His help, sometimes channeled through AA, is entirely responsible for anything I may accomplish each day. You, too, may welcome this reminder that help, freely offered and entirely undeserved, is available. Without it we were powerless and our lives can again become unmanageable. It is truly a "tranquilizer" that keeps an inflated ego under control.

These are a few of the practical working tools AA offers to bolster your desire to stay sober. Oft-times the mere repetition of these phrases will tranquilize unstable emotions and suggest better thinking. Later on, they may suggest more serious meditation.

These reminders are suggestions for you. They can be useful. Time and time again you will hear from AAs that they were able to recall these thoughts in moments of crisis, with truly wonderful results. When in need of a "tranquilizer" take one of these. When disturbed by the thought of a drink, these reminders can give you a good thought to replace a harmful one. They are simple but powerful remedies.

LISTENING AND LEARNING
January 2008

When I was counting days, I heard a lot of slogans, phrases, and suggestions that didn't make sense to me but are now indispensable bits of wisdom that aid in my staying sober.

Here are a few of them:

"There are only two things you need to know about a Higher Power: 1) That there is a power greater than yourself, and 2) You aren't it!" This was a tough one for me. I didn't think I was playing God; I was just trying to "get it together," and that meant I had to control a thing or two.

To help me get over the control hump, AAs said: "When you turn it over, don't forget to let it go, or you'll be hanging upside-down, holding on." Along with that was: "When you get to the end of your rope, let go. God will catch you." This was pretty tough for somebody who didn't believe in God or a Higher Power. I asked my sponsor how he could believe in this claptrap, and he asked me if I could control my drinking. I allowed that I couldn't control it, and he asked me if booze wasn't more powerful than I. Yes, I agreed. Alcohol was more powerful than my will, and therefore it was a power greater than myself. This left me wide open, so he asked if I could believe that there might be some benevolent power, greater than myself, that I could put my faith in.

So, I began to have faith in doorknobs. He didn't care what it was, just so long as it wasn't me, and that I attempted to imagine a loving, benevolent Higher Power to which I could turn over my life. That first attempt at having a positive power, greater than myself, has continued to expand through the years. Today, I believe that I have always had faith—sometimes negative, but faith nonetheless. At first, I had faith that everything was going to get messed up in my life, that the world was out to get me, and that I was screwed from the beginning. This faith, combined with the faith that booze would make things better, served me well—for a while. Whenever I was proven right about the rotten state of affairs, I got to drinking and believing in the power of alcohol.

My sponsor was very devious about this belief mechanism. I often argued that maybe there wasn't a Higher Power—it was all a hoax. He suggested that I retire from the debating society and act as if there were a loving God out there. He told me that I was intelligent, that I'd come to the conclusion that there was no God, and that my belief in a lack of a Higher Power was proved every day.

But, he said, "If you believed there was a loving God and you acted as if there were one, your life would be much different. And if, at the end of your life, having believed in a power greater than yourself, you found that there was none, would you care? You'd have lived a full, happy life, believing in a fictitious God, but what would it matter if it wasn't true? You would have had a happy life anyway."

I couldn't argue with that, and it gave me a kind of con-artist hope that I could put one over on this cold world. Then he encouraged me to put one over on myself, as well. "Acting As If" has served me well because it gets me "Into Action."

"Keep the Focus on Yourself" was one saying I couldn't grasp for a long time. It was similar to "It's None of Your Business What People Think of You." As difficult as this was to understand, it helped me to see that if I quit worrying about my reputation, I could spend that energy on becoming who I was supposed to be—in God's eyes. By keeping the focus on myself, I quit playing God and, therefore, diminished my judgment of others. There's a phrase in the Big Book that says that an alcoholic is not qualified to judge anybody, and that, too, is liberating. If I can get myself to see that I'm not qualified to judge, then I can leave that job to my Higher Power and get back to being me.

"To Thine Own Self Be True" had me stumped. I thought I'd been true to myself when I was selfishly going after whatever I wanted when I drank. But I was being true to my alcoholism, not myself. As I did the Steps, and I got past the Fifth Step, I began to see that if I could accept myself as I was, I could then allow myself to be me. By not violating myself with booze and destructive behavior, I saw that I could do the things I'd always wanted to do but felt unworthy, unqualified, and too scared to try.

I would also hear: "If you want to know how you're doing, ask your sponsor." I wondered what kind of idiot came up with that. I figured there was a subgroup of AA using it as a tool to get me to relinquish control over my life. How would a sponsor know how I was doing? I got upset at this, but AAs would patiently explain that I was inside the experience and unable to know how well I was doing.

In addition, I had little experience with doing things that weren't self-destructive. My sponsor spelled it out for me: "To build self-esteem, you have to do estimable acts." That was when I knew he was nuts, but he told me that building self-esteem was so foreign to me that I wouldn't know what it felt like.

So, every time that I did something different than I'd done before— not lie, avoid a fight, let something go—I'd feel awful. I would go to him, asking what was up. He would listen to me and then pronounce that I'd just done an estimable act, and that's why I felt like crap. Huh?

He explained that it was the exact opposite of my normal behavior and I didn't have a "sober reference" for it, so it was normal for me to feel uncomfortable. And that was why I had to ask my sponsor how I was doing—I couldn't tell on my own.

There's a lot more that I learned as a newcomer—things I still use today to fit myself to maximum service to my fellows. The basics work regardless of the amount of time anyone has sober. Alcoholism is relieved of its power when honesty, open-mindedness, and willingness combine within me to change my question from "Why?" to "How?" Then, I can get into the stream of life and out of my own way.

NICHOLAS Y.
Penngrove, California

LIVING THE SLOGANS
November 2002

In the beginning of my sobriety in 1987, the slogans of Alcoholics Anonymous meant little to this high-bottom, twenty-year-old alcoholic. Things were good; life was sweet—as long as I didn't drink. Those slogans were fine for some, and they sounded really good when I spoke them from the podium, but words to live by? I thought not. I was far too busy mapping out my life to "Let Go And Let God." In my defense, I was really good at practicing "First Things First," as long as it involved me being first. I was not a nay-sayer of the slogans of Alcoholics Anonymous, just ignorant of their meaning and power to comfort in times of difficulty.

As you can imagine, my inability to apply the slogans, or any other part of the program, led me, after a time, back into the grip of active alcoholism at the age of thirty-one. The magic elixir had me, and good! No slogans, or amount of knowledge, nor any power on this earth could stop me for the next three years, and believe me, this was not for lack of trying everything in my power to get sober.

During this time, my mother, a sober member of Alcoholics Anonymous since 1978, with twenty years of sobriety, was dying of lung cancer. I struggled to stay sober for her, to be there in her time of need. Even something as monumental as losing my mother and best friend in the world could not stop my drinking. I knew I was in trouble, and so did she. In her last week on earth, on my way home from a meeting (on one of my many failed missions to get and stay sober), I visited her in the hospital to see how she was doing and to update her on my progress with recovery.

I started to tell her that I re-hired my sponsor, whom I had fired in year five of my sobriety my first time around, and that I thought I had a good shot at staying sober this time, having also joined a new group. I had a solid plan of action. Her simple reply to my ramblings was, "Kim, what time is it?"

"Uh ... well, I think it's about 9:30, Ma. Why?" I said, somewhat confused at where she was going with this.

"Well, it's almost time for bed then, isn't it?"

"Yes," I answered, thinking that the pain medication must be kicking in again.

"Well, if you didn't drink today, and the day is almost over, then you are staying sober. Right?" I remember thinking to myself how simplistic and matter-of-fact she sounded about my foolproof plan.

"I guess I am," I said, kissing her good night, and thus putting an end to the last conversation I would ever have with my mother. She passed five days later.

It would be a nice ending to a touching story if I said I stayed away from booze from that day on, but this was not to be the case. I had to get to that jumping-off point the Big Book speaks of, and eventually I did.

I have been sober now a little over two years. My mother has been gone almost three years, yet not a day passes when I don't think about that bedside meeting that was all of four sentences long, and how the few words she said to me then have helped in keeping me sober for the past couple of years.

When I reflect on that last encounter with my mom, I realize that she was not simplistic, she was "Keeping It Simple." And although she knew her time was limited, she also knew that all any of us have, alcoholic or not, is "One Day at a Time." And despite the fact that she was gasping for every breath, she was "Passing It On" to me with the hope that I might again find sobriety. A lot has happened in these past few years, and I've had days when I didn't think I would make it through. Yet "One Day at a Time," I attend a meeting or talk to a member of AA, and thanks to people like my mom, I have a life that is not owned or threatened by alcohol.

It used to be the more elaborate and flamboyant a message was, the more I was apt to listen. That is not the case any longer. I don't just hear the slogans anymore; I feel them when I speak them, usually out loud, in times of crisis. They take hold of me; they change the course of my day if I let them. Imagine that! Those cute little banners with the little words on them that we use to decorate the halls of AA can change my day! Who would have thought? Thanks to those cute little banners, I don't do much of that thinking stuff anymore if I can help it.

KIM R.
Fairhaven, Massachusetts

OUR MEETINGS: COMING HOME TOGETHER

Where the transforming spirit moves among us

Everybody knows what an ordinary meeting in the day-to-day world is like. But only AA members know what *our* meetings mean to us. Known for their ability to transform church basements into sanctuaries, AA meetings are, in the words of a former Grapevine editor, "those magical gatherings where the transforming spirit of Alcoholics Anonymous moves among us, bringing sobriety to those who desire it, and enhancing it for those who already have it."

In "One for the Ages," a member young enough to have never had a legal drink recounts a happy memory about celebrating her twenty-first birthday ... sober. Not surprisingly, it was at a meeting of her home group, a place of rare safety, where she was inspired to relive and share that private memory. This story also describes an unusual, informal, and very effective "meeting," held by young people at the movies.

Why would AA meetings be valuable in jails and prisons? A story written from inside, "Playing a Vital Part," explains. "As one who definitely needs the program, I believe that our meetings have a tendency to stabilize the insecure, encourage the timid to speak up and the over-boastful to be less boastful and, for the problem drinker, the program at least starts him thinking. The therapeutic value of AA is unquestionable."

"I would like to share about an incredible journey I completed last year," begins the story, "Don't Forget the Cookies," as the author describes his personal journey as he reaches to complete his goal of attending every meeting in the St. Louis area.

The differences in meetings were fascinating, he reports. The meetings' similarities, which he could count on wherever he went, he found to be trustworthy and deeply moving.

WELCOME TO LEETOWN
June 2006

I have been in AA for over 16 years and have experienced the Fellowship in the four states I have lived in during that time: California, Florida, Virginia, and West Virginia. Early on, ever since I heard about "greeters," a service position in which one or more persons have the "job" of welcoming people as they walk into the meeting, I've always thought this a wonderful way to start any meeting. Let's face it, some of us walk into meetings scared, depressed, angry, or overwhelmed. We need a welcome. No place is this welcome warmer than the Step meeting that takes place every Tuesday night in Leetown, West Virginia.

I have attended the Leetown AA group off and on in the 11 years since I arrived in West Virginia, and my experience is always the same. The people are so darn nice, they make me want to keep coming back. So I do, and every time, more than half the room says hello, says goodbye, tells me the meeting is glad to have me, tells me the meeting needs me, or that it's just plain old great to see me. Even if they just saw me last week. Some offer a hug, most offer a warm handshake, others just say it with a smile. It's AA hospitality at its finest.

Leaving the meeting one Tuesday night, I was filled with warmth thinking about the members' hospitality and decency, thinking about the strength of their home group and their sobriety, and thinking about how they are walking the talk, so to speak, and I was overcome with gratitude upon realizing how fond I had become of the group. I then realized—with some irony—how the Leetown group was a lot like that television comedy "Cheers," where camaraderie grows and, as the theme song says, "Everybody knows your name." That's exactly how it is in Leetown.

Leetown is no longer a bunch of drunks telling war stories around the bar over beers; they are a bunch of sober individuals sharing their messages of recovery, sanity, and hope around tables in church basements. Instead of alcohol, they drink coffee or some other nonalcoholic beverage. Instead of talking about what they're gonna do someday, they speak about what they've done and share their experience and strength so others can do it, too. And instead of stumbling out of the bar bleary-eyed at the end of the night (or being escorted out with a loud, "And don't come back!"), they are looking people like me in the eye and saying, with sincerity, that they are glad I am here and they hope I will keep coming back.

I can only imagine the effect their brand of hospitality has on newcomers. I'd say that's a powerful example of how it works because recovery can't really begin until the fellowship part is in place. It's also a good reminder, as one of our sayings goes, to "let it begin with me."

KATHERINE C.
Charles Town, West Virginia

DON'T FORGET THE COOKIES
April 2010

I would like to share about an incredible journey I completed last year. Several years ago, I'd noticed some changes to my home group meeting and to other nearby meetings that I felt were significant. Fewer people were arriving early and staying after the meeting to help out, fewer people were showing concern for visitors and newcomers, and fewer people were attending AA service functions. I didn't know if I was becoming a "Bleeding Deacon," if I wasn't communicating the things I felt were important, or if AA was changing in a new way without my permission.

I decided to go to a few meetings that I hadn't been to in a while and that was very satisfying. So I went to a few more, and then to a few others that were new to me—out of my comfort zone. Then, at some point, I decided to attend every meeting in the St. Louis Area's "Where and When" meeting list. With the exception of most closed womens' meetings, I achieved my goal. I attended 721 meetings across 16 districts; it took more than two years. (I was able to attend one or two closed womens' meetings when they were hosting an open potluck dinner or other gathering, but decided to leave most of those meetings alone. In hindsight, I might have contacted those groups, introduced myself and asked to be a guest.)

My journey started in 2006 and ended in January 2009. My home group has been vital to me through my 22 years of sobriety, and I missed mine two to four times per month. I also sacrificed most of my paid time off from work to attend meetings. I went to meetings during most holidays, sacrificed being with family and friends, and missed other AA activities. Some meetings were more than 80 miles away, and I spent one or two hours just driving there. I spent untold dollars filling my gas tank and had to buy three new tires. At times I was getting my oil changed every month.

I attended morning, noon, afternoon, evening and midnight meetings. They were open, closed, male, mixed, smoking and non-smoking. They were held mostly at churches; I felt like I entered every type of church known to attend a meeting. Additionally, I attended meetings at hospitals, treatment centers, veteran's administration centers, grade schools, high schools, colleges, central service offices, clubs, facilities, halfway houses, government centers, public libraries, recreational centers, hotels, bowling alleys and parks.

Each district had large meetings and small ones, but attendance was mostly between 10 and 30 people. The coffee house had the best coffee, but it wasn't free. I usually brought my own coffee, however. I stumbled into a handful of potluck dinners, usually when I was hungry and broke. Meeting formats included reading from the Big Book, *Twelve Steps and Twelve Traditions*, *As Bill Sees It*, Grapevine and AA pamphlets. There were topic and discussion meetings that used AA materials, and "topic sticks" and "grab bag" formats, where each person had a different sobriety topic to discuss. There were Step meetings, Tradition meetings, inventory meetings, meditation meetings and some that incorporated Al-Anon into the meeting.

I attended meetings at which I was the only man there. I also attended meetings where I was the only white male, heterosexual male or English-speaking male; the only one who didn't ride a Harley Davidson to the meeting; the only one under 65, or over 21; the best off financially, or the least well-off.

There were four things, I think, that made a group stand out from the other 720 meetings. I used the acronym ACES to identify them. First, members Acknowledged the newcomers and visitors. I felt much more comfortable when someone came up before the meeting and welcomed me warmly. Second was Candy, Cookies or Cake. Providing some type of munchies costs so little compared to one night at a bar, nightclub or courtroom. The third thing was Excitement. The group members seemed excited about sobriety and "absolutely insist(ed) on enjoying life." Finally, they were participating in the Service Structure, were part of the AA community and Fellowship by having someone attend the monthly district, area or intergroup meeting, and by supporting the service structure financially or by volunteering.

I met AA members whom I called "ambassadors" of AA, using the same ACES acronym. The ambassadors were Accountable; they always attended their home group meeting, they had a sponsor, and they worked the Twelve Steps and Traditions. They showed Care and Concern for those around them before, during and after the meeting. They didn't go directly to their favorite AA buddies prior to the meeting, or include only them throughout the meeting. They avoided being snobbish or judgmental of others. Thirdly, they were Examples of the AA solution. And finally, they were Speaking "the language of the heart." They weren't lecturing or trying to educate others; they weren't trying to entertain or put on a show; and they weren't trying to prove that they had the worst alcoholic bottom ever. They didn't talk down to others, belittle them or point out their shortcomings. They just shared what was in their hearts, not their heads.

As I attended more and more meetings over the last couple of years, I felt and saw how much better these things made a person and a group. Going by what I've seen and experienced, an alcoholic, myself included, can be driven by ego and be highly selfish and self-centered. Now I'm trying harder than ever in my home group to talk only about my own strengths, hopes and experiences. They aren't an opinion; they are what I feel. I'm trying to talk only about myself and not you or "some people." I'm trying to be an ACES member, with an ACES home group.

BRIAN K.
St. Louis, Missouri

ONE FOR THE AGES
September 2005

I've never taken a legal drink. By the grace of my Higher Power and with the help of my fellow AAs I know today that I don't ever have to. I'm nearly 27 in calendar years now, and almost seven years sober. At my home group meeting last night, I was reminded of one of my happiest memories: my twenty-first birthday, and how I celebrated it sober.

Somewhere around age ten, about a year before my first drink, I found a perpetual calendar and figured out that my twenty-first birthday would fall on a Saturday. I had daydreamed about throwing the party of the millennium ever since, a grand and glorious affair that would be attended by all the friends and admirers I would surely have picked up by then. That fantasy persisted until, at age nineteen, I found myself in the rooms of Alcoholics Anonymous.

I picked up a one-year chip at the age of 20 years and nine months. As my birthday approached, I wrestled with the idea of getting drunk to celebrate my adulthood, then immediately returning to AA. I rationalized that my group would love me anyway (and they would have), and told myself that it was perfectly normal to get drunk on one's twenty-first birthday. I knew that many people who get drunk never make it back, and the insanity of my behavior during my last drunk had landed me in a locked psych ward, perilously close to being involuntarily committed. But, of course, I could get sober again if I wanted to, right?

As the big day came closer, I shared openly in a meeting that I was feeling ambivalent about missing out on my chance to walk into a bar and prove my adulthood by getting legally drunk. An old playmate, whose twenty-first birthday would come just three weeks after mine, encouraged this. She wanted to be there for my birthday and have me join her in the celebration of hers.

An AA friend told me that she loved me and wanted to help me celebrate my birthday, but that could only happen if it was a sober occasion. She suggested that I let her make the birthday plans and concentrate on staying sober today. I knew that she was a much better friend than I deserved, and she certainly had what I wanted in a way that the old playmate did not, so I agreed.

At 4:00 on the afternoon of my birthday, I arrived at our meeting hall to find her there with several other AAs, all people that I really liked and whose sobriety I respected. Mike H., the longest-sober member, said that we had to help another alcoholic as a way of showing our gratitude that my Higher Power was giving me a sober coming-of-age. So, we caravanned to the house of a newcomer he was sponsoring, a guy he said was really struggling to feel like he belonged in AA. The slightly shocked-looking fellow answered his door to find half a dozen AAs on his doorstep and nearly fainted when his sponsor instructed him to change his clothes and join us.

They took me to see a movie that was probably more appropriate for a twelve-year-old than an adult (I was dying to see it at the time), and certainly not anything this group of sober, mature adults would have chosen if they were thinking about themselves. Phone calls were made, word spread, and by the time we arrived at the restaurant for dinner, our group was over a dozen strong. We took over several tables and talked for hours. I asked to hear about their twenty-first birthdays, and I began to realize what a gift they'd given me when most of them could only say, "Holly, I don't really remember."

When I got back to my little apartment that night, I cried myself to sleep, but they were tears of gratitude and joy. That was the happiest birthday of my life, and the first time I ever felt really loved by a large group of friends. Like many alcoholics, I'd always been good at faking a sense of ease in a group, but in reality I was usually ready to jump out of my skin and get back to the comfort of my liquid self-pity. The love, friendship, and language of the heart I experienced that night cemented my desire to surrender not just to sobriety, but to the AA way of life.

Today, I understand what a gift it is that I got sober so early in my life. I try to give back by tangible acts of kindness that say, "You are important" to newcomers. I want them to see that the AA way of life and the relationships we build in recovery are gifts in and of themselves, even beyond the all-important gift of staying sober one day at a time.

My friend with the birthday three weeks after mine? She e-mailed me a photo from her twenty-first a couple of days after the fact. She was passed out on the sidewalk in front of a bar. Her big brother had talked her into dyeing her hair purple. At least, she thinks it was him. She doesn't remember.

I'm still saving her a chair.

HOLLY H.
Huntsville, Alabama

PLAYING A VITAL PART
May 1960

It is often asked, "What earthly good is AA in prison?" To this I can only say that we build the foundation of good living while we are here in the hopes that some day, upon our release from here, we can put this knowledge into effect and never again come back to one of these places. Of course, some of us stumble and come back, only because we have missed the boat along the line. But if we take the program seriously and work it into our lives according to the Twelve

Suggested Steps, in the long run, we will succeed.

Since its inception at this unit, Alcoholics Anonymous has been of definite rehabilitative value in our midst. AA has not only proved to be one of our greatest morale builders but we also find that AA meets a need for a specific type of therapy that was lacking for us prior to AA.

Most inmates attending have an element of humility about them. Some members of the group originally carried a chip on their shoulders and were bitter at the whole world. Now they seem to have the appearance of persons who have discarded a whole burden.

As one who definitely needs the program, I believe that our meetings have a tendency to stabilize the insecure, encourage the timid to speak up and the over-boastful to be less boastful and, for the problem drinker, the program at least starts him thinking. The therapeutic value of AA is unquestionable. Our meetings are occasions for an exchange of ideas. AA's philosophy develops sincerity, understanding, and even brotherly love.

We are proud of our AA program and extremely grateful for the assistance rendered by the various AA groups in the different towns, cities, units and other institutions.

J. D. W.
Huntsville, Texas

LOST AT SEA? NOT ME *(from Dear Grapevine)*
June 2001

When I left New York in 1998 on what I hope will be a circumnavigation of the globe aboard a sailboat, I brought the AA International Directory with me, but I had no clue as to what to expect. The first person to greet us at the Customs Dock in Bermuda was someone I later met at a meeting. He kindly drove me to several meetings, including those at a convention there.

Since then, I've met countless AA members and found my way to meetings almost everywhere we've stopped. When none are listed in the Directory, I find a phone book, a church, or ask the police. And I keep in touch by e-mail with people like the one I met at a meeting at a marina in Trinidad started by a former "yachtie." I've also made a little flag bearing a symbol that members in the Fellowship recognize.

At present, I'm near some uninhabited islands off Panama. But recently I attended a meeting in Vermont, where I was visiting my daughter. When I introduced myself and explained that I was sailing around the world, the leader paused and asked, "Aren't you a little lost?"

"I'm never lost at an AA meeting," I replied, "and for that, I am most grateful."

SALLY J.

STARK-RAVING SOBER INTO CYBERSPACE
June 2003

In 1997, I had not picked up a drink in eight years, but I had not been to meetings in several years either. I was in a bad marriage and stark-raving sober! I knew something had to change before I picked up that first drink, but I was scared to death to go back to face-to-face meetings. I'd hung around AA for the first few years, attending meetings if I had time, always arriving just as the meeting was starting, and being the first one out the door and into my car when the meeting was over. Then I discovered the wonderful world of the Internet and stumbled upon AA online one sleepless night. Eventually I ended up in a womens' e-mail group, and that's where my recovery and new life finally began.

AAW14 was a wonderful group of approximately twenty women. The elected chair would post a topic via e-mail once a week and throughout the week we would respond to the topic, or with anything else that was on our minds. It gave me a chance to read up on a Step or topic before I responded, and the women gave me the courage to go back to face-to-face meetings, slowly but surely.

However, the greatest gift they gave me was friendship. I had friends in Australia, New Zealand, and all over the United States who made me laugh and made me cry. I remember one gal who came into our group as an active alcoholic. She'd stay in touch, go to meetings, and then relapse. Then we no longer heard from her, and I still think of her. Another gal kept us informed as she and her family survived the wrath of a hurricane in Alabama. Another wrote the most fascinating responses, and I wanted what she had. It turned out she lived only four hours from me, so eventually we met and I asked her to be my sponsor. Soon, I was doing service work, sponsoring, attending consistent meetings—and eventually, switching to a sponsor I could see at meetings.

Today I have a wonderful home group and more friends than I ever imagined possible. I have held the same service commitment in my Intergroup for the past three years, and have a sense of peace within myself made possible only by a power greater than myself.

ROXIE H.
Taylor, Michigan

THE WINNER'S GUIDE TO BORING MEETINGS
May 1984

For a brief period during my fifth year of continuous sobriety, I was going through a rough patch in my attendance at AA meetings. Somehow, the drinking stories and the tales of the early days of AA were rubbing me the wrong way. If I wasn't bored, I was angry. What to do?

Leave the Fellowship altogether? I had heard enough people say that they came to meetings to find out what happens to alcoholics who don't come to meetings. It wouldn't be quitting—I'd be allowing others to drive me out!

Change my patterns of attendance? I tried attending different groups and different types of meetings. That did help somewhat, but a complete change of groups made me feel that I was a beginner again, trying to break into new friendship circles. The loneliness I felt when I cut myself off from my familiar AA associates was not helping my mental health. I was still bored with "identification meetings" full of drunk stories, and there weren't enough Step, Big Book study, or discussion groups near enough to where I live and work.

Trying to solve my own problem by running from the Fellowship or my regular meetings was a dry-drunk manifestation of my alcoholic pattern of running from my problems. Resentments were building up inside me, and I was keeping it all inside. If I didn't want to relapse into the active form of our disease of alcoholism, what should I do?

The answer, of course, was to talk about my feelings. My first opportunity came at a "problem-study group," which I went to with the specific intent of letting it all out. It wasn't hard to do. I almost exploded as my anguish, pain, frustration, hostility, and confusion poured forth, complete with table-banging and language that would make a strip-joint bouncer blush.

The assembled members listened patiently to my distress, then offered some opinions on what they had done in similar circumstances. Here was a definition of our Fellowship in action. By sharing their experience, strength, and hope with me, they saved me, so I have been able to pass these ideas on to others trying to work the program.

Some of their suggestions included ways to occupy my mind during boring or repetitive drunkalogs. One urged me to count the words on the Steps or Traditions banner or, better yet, to examine how each Step has been accomplished in my life. Another suggestion was to use the time to take my daily or weekly inventory, making a mental list of those to whom I must promptly admit my errors. Still another bit of advice was to use the time to meditate on the word "one" or the word "unity" until I could see how I and the person speaking were similar.

The suggestion I liked best, however, and the one I subsequently practiced for six months with great, lasting benefit, was to carry a little notebook to meetings and write down any pieces of AA folk wisdom that might be lurking in the midst of otherwise uninteresting stories. At first, I was self-conscious about jotting down those pithy gems, but no one seemed to mind, and my collection grew rapidly. It was like finding gold nuggets amid rocks in the stream of consciousness.

The first saying I noted started me off in the right frame of mind: "What I don't know about this program may kill me." That was followed closely by "The clenched fist never receives" and "It's AA or 'amen' for me." After a while, I heard statements like "I don't live for AA—I use AA to live," "If you want sobriety, you must go among those who have it," and "If you want what we have, then do what we do."

Soon, my notebook was overflowing with those statements that we pass on to each other as part of the message of recovery. I learned to look at people and the way that they are handling this program of living. I learned that it is the simple, easily remembered statements that are our most eloquent contributions to one another.

To be teachable, I had to be reachable. I can see now that my stinking thinking was leading to drinking. Since the door swings both ways in AA, I had come to a turning point where I had to hang on and let go. My confidence today is gained from my humility of yesterday. Now, I go to meetings not to be entertained but to be healed, and I continue to stay around to witness the naturally occurring miracles as we love each other into well-being.

Today, I know that notes in the same key resonate together. I'm at meetings to give as well as to receive. No matter how much continuous sobriety I have to my and AA's credit, I am still only one drink away from a drunk, just like everybody else in these meeting rooms. If there's any message in all of this problem-turned-project, it can perhaps be summed up in these words heard at an otherwise dreary meeting: "I never let the seeds stop me from eating the watermelon."

C. F.
Wollstonecraft

IT WORKS IN ALL OUR AFFAIRS

AA is far more than the sum of its parts

Alcoholics Anonymous is definitely far more than the sum of its parts. There's a reason why we don't think of AA as merely a recovery club. Or a group. Or an affiliation. When we decide that we are AA members, we both enter a program and are received into a Fellowship, enabling even the most tempest-tossed of us to build not only a new life, but an entirely different *way of living.*

It's often amazing how one element of our program dovetails neatly into another. "Welcome to a New Life," a story from Bolivia, begins with the writer sailing along in sobriety for over two years—until she finds herself stuck in a dysfunctional, irresponsible home group, and is beset by familiar old negative thoughts and gossipy tendencies. Because she handles it soberly, this rift ultimately results in a fresh new meeting in a more affordable area of town that is hungry for recovery, and she soon finds AA working its miracles in all her affairs.

An editorial written when AA was just a few years old, "On Living the AA Way for Seven Years," recounts the editor's difficulty in understanding how members go through terrible trouble with their sobriety intact—till he was confronted with such troubles himself.

In "OK in My Skin," the writer admits he was afraid he would be asked to leave local meetings because he was gay, so he drives an hour to a meeting where no one knows him. "I remember that night feeling for the first time in my life that I fit in somewhere."

A former Benedictine monk describes how he came to AA at the age of 69 after alcoholism destroyed everything that meant anything to him, in "An Ex-Monk Picks Up the Pieces." Through a well-worked program and our Fellowship, everything this monk has lost—anything any of us has thrown away in the throes of our disease—is given back, new, improved, and appreciated.

MORNING WISHES
May 1960

To be sober this day and live it as though it might be the last.

1. To have a few friends who understand me and yet remain my friends.
2. To sense the presence of God—as I understand him.
3. To have an objective today—constructive work that requires time and effort.
4. To have an understanding heart, which is always one beat from eternity.
5. To have moments of leisure—time to restore emotions, regain humility and peace of mind.
6. To have a mind unafraid to travel, even though the trail be not blazed; but let me avoid egotistical pretensions and delusions of grandeur.
7. To have an occasional sight of the eternal hills and the unresting sea, and of something beautiful the hand of man has made.
8. To have the power to laugh, but let me be considerate, tolerant and respecting the dignity of all persons—to each his own, void of criticism.
9. To do nothing at the expense of others.
10. To have the grace to listen with patience to other people's troubles, but let me forget my own. Instead of envy, hate, despise, deceive, resent, and begrudge, let me approve, respect and admire.
11. To have the patience to wait for the coming of these things—with the wisdom to know when they come.

J. M.
San Diego, California

WELCOME TO A NEW LIFE
(Published in La Viña) May/June 2010

I came to AA for the same reason everybody comes—to do something about the way I drank. Although alcohol had not yet stolen my family, my job, or my profession, it had stripped me of my right to be happy. Alcohol subjected my life to a dangerous diet of negative thoughts and feelings toward myself and others. I was on an endless path of self-destruction, leading to nowhere during the eight or more years of my alcohol use.

One blessed day, with just enough awareness that mine was not a normal way of life, I searched in the local phone book for Alcoholics Anonymous, after learning about AA at a work-related public information meeting. The voice on the other side of the line exuded calm and peace and patiently listened to me, finally responding with "Welcome to a new life, if you want it," and then offering an explanation of the disease of alcoholism and the purpose of AA.

I knew immediately that I had the disease, and that I had to decide whether or not to continue suffering, blaming everything and everyone else, or to accept who I was and begin to work for what I wanted to become.

Seven years and a few months have passed since I chose AA after that phone call, and I feel deep down that it was the best decision of my life. I entered AA by joining my neighborhood's group, and my new life began to emerge, a life without alcohol.

That's when my real story began, the story I want to share.

I did quite a lot of service during the first two years of my recovery, and time went by calmly and happily. It wasn't until my third year of abstinence from alcohol that I felt something was missing. I did not return to drinking, because I had no desire for it, but my life returned to what it had been—negative.

Again I felt possessed by destructive, often arrogant thoughts. What was missing? I wondered. What have I not done? Or, what was I doing wrong? I could not ask a sponsor, since I had not considered a sponsor to be necessary, believing that the only requirement was to stop drinking.

My third and fourth years came and went with more grief than glory. I attracted the negative in everything—my personal relationships, my family, my work. Of course, I blamed my Higher Power, the circumstances, other people, even my country. My attitude and character became unbearable even to me. I would get angry quickly and would shout and swear. I was intolerant and a gossiper. My AA group and my service position were excuses for me to attack or make fun of my fellows. The truth is that I had a sick dependence on what others said or did.

My motto was that if others had not said or done what they said or did, I would not have reacted, so therefore they were to blame. After all, I had done what I was supposed to do. I had stopped drinking.

During my fifth year, our group suffered a hard blow when we irresponsibly rented a place beyond our budget. At the same time our prudent reserve was stolen by a member. We ended up with nothing but a luxurious meeting space that we couldn't afford. Elected as general service coordinator, but without any idea of what that meant, I managed to hide my shame as I approached a fellow from another group who had performed the same service.

We met, and the first thing he asked was, "Do you have a sponsor?" I casually answered no. "Do you work the Steps?" was his next question. Well, we read the Steps at each meeting, but beyond the First Step, I had never given them much importance. I said I knew them, because after all I had five years in AA, but do I work them? No. He smiled and said, "How about we start there?"

I started working the Steps that day, encouraged by the fellow I just happened to ask for advice, who became my sponsor. In the Steps I found the answers to my questions, discovered what was missing, and realized what I had to do. Slowly I realized that AA was not just about stopping drinking; that was just the beginning. The essential next step was to build a new life through a spiritual awakening. As I found and felt a Higher Power, my thoughts began to turn positive, and I experienced joy and acceptance. Yes, I wanted dependence, but a dependence on a Higher Power.

I shared my experience with the members of the steering committee of my group, and thus was born a chain of sponsorships and Step study that extended to the Traditions and the Concepts.

What times those were! We worked hard on our personal recovery and also on the recovery of the group. Soon we began to feel and live the great AA principles of anonymity, sponsorship and rotation, to name a few.

Not everyone in the group agreed with our efforts, believing that putting down the drink was all that mattered. What started as a controversy turned into verbal attacks as well as insults and personal aggressions. Incredibly though, these disagreements led to something wonderful happening. A new group was born. What better reason could we need to start a new meeting of our own, so our community could grow and expand this great AA program?

We jumped eagerly into the creation of a new group, choosing to meet in a sector of town where the need for Alcoholics Anonymous was real and serious. This has been the most beautiful experience I have lived, to this day. We decided to call our new meeting The Language of the Heart, because it offers us the same love we feel when we open the book with that title.

The Language of the Heart is now more than eight months old, and we have many members, the majority being women and young men, all practicing the Steps with their sponsors. It is no exaggeration to say that every time I open the door I think, What an atmosphere of love and peace breathes here! And I thank my Higher Power that I am a part of it.

Today I look back at my life and I am grateful for being who I am now and for everything I have experienced, because if I were not an alcoholic, I would not be living this life called sobriety.

At the moment, my family circumstances require my presence, so I have had to temporarily move away from service in the AA community. In making that decision, I am living what our Twelfth Step so wisely suggests: practicing my recovery program in all my affairs. And, boy, am I doing it! I am grateful every day for it, too.

NINOSKA T.
La Paz, Bolivia

ON THE MOVE *(from Dear Grapevine)*
October 2010

I would like the Grapevine to have a monthly or yearly feature on the topic of moving in sobriety. I've seen many people struggle with this; they move, go to a few meetings, don't really connect, isolate and start drinking again.

I have struggled myself, specifically, when the new area is so different that I'm unable to find my footing. What worked for me was becoming a general service representative (as counter-intuitive as it seems), picking some meetings and going to them every week, sticking my hand out, and hearing what other people did that worked. I also think that it would be healing for people to write about what they did that didn't work. I've seen this emerge as a "special need" in AA and I want to see how we can be there for the struggling alcoholics in this situation.

MAIA L.
Dublin, California

OK IN MY SKIN
February 2011

Growing up in rural Indiana, I never planned on being an alcoholic any more than I planned on being gay.

I had a relatively normal childhood. I was the next to last of five kids. My dad worked in a factory and my mother was a homemaker. When I was 2 or 3 my mom would lie down with me for my nap. After I got her to sleep I would get up and do all the things she wouldn't let me do. One day I had a cough. She was asleep but I remembered her saying I could have some cough syrup. I couldn't reach it, so I climbed up on a chair and onto the kitchen cabinets until I could get to that bottle of cherry-flavored codeine cough syrup—yum. I drank the whole thing. My memory fades after that, but I'm told my grandparents had to help take care of me because I talked nonstop for three days and nights.

Because my dad had not gone to college, we were told early on that to be successful in life we needed a good education and that going to college was required. Fear was my constant companion. I remember making myself sick with worry every year when school started and I would think of all of the possibilities for things to go wrong. What if the teacher hated me or nobody talked to me? What if supplies cost too much, or I didn't get good grades? I was painfully shy but wanted to be the center of attention, and I always strove to be the teacher's pet. I needed that; I wanted to feel special. Other kids seemed happy and confident and I wanted that, but I didn't know how to get there. I always felt as if I had been dropped into the wrong household. My interests seemed out of sync with my siblings and almost everyone I knew. I had realized I was gay somewhere between ages 10 and 12, but I knew I couldn't tell anyone.

Around that time, there was a party at our house and my siblings and I were allowed to drink. My parents thought that if we drank at home we would learn to be responsible drinkers; it sounded like it would work. I got very drunk, vomited and was hungover, but I liked it. However, I didn't really start drinking heavily until I was 18.

I got in trouble when law enforcement friends of my father told him what I was doing. I tried to quit but I couldn't. My parents asked, "How could you do this to us?" I didn't see that I was doing anything to them; I just wanted that comfortable numbness.

There was very little, if any, information that was gay-positive back then, and there was certainly nothing on TV—no celebrities could risk coming out. In high school, I hung with the druggies, so no one cared if I didn't date girls. My grades and my attitude were terrible, but I managed to graduate and because of my SAT scores I got into college.

I started to meet others who were gay, and drinking was a huge part of our subculture. I was 18 when I met my first partner, who was 26. He owned his own business and supplied me with all the alcohol I wanted. I pretty much stopped taking anything else but alcohol. That seemed to make my parents and my partner happy, and I could drink as much as I wanted. In the beginning he made me feel special and, for the first time in my life, attractive. I didn't realize that his drinking was a problem as well.

What followed were several years of an emotionally abusive relationship, but I assumed this was probably as good as it would get. I decided to go back to college and thought then I would feel OK about myself. The last semester that I drank I was on the dean's list. I worked full-time and I just assumed, due to my lack of self-esteem, that if I could do it, a well-trained chimp could do it. I was miserable, trapped in a sick relationship, and my life seemed hopeless. I don't know that I actually wanted to die; I was just so tired of hurting.

I believe now that a Higher Power led me to AA, through a series of people. My life was unmanageable. I didn't think I was bad enough to need to go to AA meetings, though. I feared that people in AA would know I was gay and make me leave. I was too afraid to go to meetings in the town I lived in, so I drove an hour to a meeting in Indianapolis. It was the only meeting of gays in AA in the state back then. I stopped drinking in November 1980 but didn't go to AA until late January 1981. I remember that night feeling for the first time in my life that I fit in somewhere.

I reluctantly got a sponsor, Larry, and off and on for the next 28 years until his death, he played an important part in my life. He spent lots of time teaching me about AA and the structure of the program. He took me to AA meetings until I was less afraid and could go by myself. He showed me how he worked the Steps in his daily life, and I am sure he saved my life. He helped me to become honest and to check my motives, to learn that it did no good to do a good deed just to try and manipulate the outcome. When it was time for my six-month token I was a mess. My life was awful and I just had to take peoples' word that it would get better. The night before my anniversary, Larry gave me a bronze token in an envelope and told me that if I could stay sober until midnight, I could open it. Even though it was a school night, I stayed up late just so I could have that token.

After one or two years Larry was laid off and moved to Indianapolis to find work. He suggested my second sponsor, a woman named Eunice. Larry and Eunice didn't appear to be afraid of anybody or anything. I wanted that. Through AA I learned to trust a Higher Power and eventually myself. The Promises say that if we work the Steps, fear of people and economic insecurity will leave us, and it does. I joke that I went to the Larry and Eunice School of Assertiveness Training. I could never repay the kindness and strength given to me by these and other people in AA. I learned from the straight people in AA in Muncie, Ind., to love who I am, that I did not have to take flak from people because I happened to be born gay. They taught me that I was perfectly acceptable just the way God made me.

There were those who didn't like me because I was gay. Some would tell Eunice, "It's OK that he's gay, but does he have to talk?" This was followed by the air turning blue—she could cuss like a sail-

or. Many of them nevertheless learned to respect me for staying sober and living a good, honest life. One of the most important lessons I learned in AA was not to care so much about what others thought of me. I was told I wouldn't worry so much about what they thought of me if I realized how little they thought of me. Eunice remained my sponsor for about the next 16 or 17 years. She eventually ended up in a nursing home and died without ever taking another drink.

In 1987 I met my current partner, a non-drinker. Relationships aren't easy for me. We have grown up together and spent a lot of time around the program of AA. While our relationship is not perfect, I am so grateful that he and his family are a part of my life.

If anyone had told me 30 years ago that my life would be like it is now I would not have believed him. If I had been able to decide what I wanted instead of what my Higher Power wanted, I would have vastly shortchanged myself. I didn't really believe that happiness was real or possible for me. I didn't know that I didn't have to drink; that I didn't have to live in fear. I didn't know that I could feel this OK in my own skin.

DAN S.
Indianapolis, Indiana

AN EX-MONK PICKS UP THE PIECES
October 2008

I came to AA at the age of 69 and will soon be 79. My sobriety date is August 9, 1999.

My alcoholism started late in my life when, at the age of 40, I bought my first bottle of bourbon and proceeded to pickle my dead spirit in alcohol for the next 30 years. I had just legally left my Benedictine monastery after 20 years of service and the Catholic priesthood after 15 years. The separation was extremely traumatic. In today's slang, my life sucked. Alcohol would help me forget it all!

By the time I came to AA, I was retired after 25 years of education, a postgraduate degree, 30 years of teaching, and 40 years of supervision and management experience. Over the years I had become a high-class wino, drinking close to a gallon a day. I had no problems with the law, my wife was still with me, and I paid my bills and taxes.

My alcoholism, however, had destroyed the priceless intangibles: a sense of values and meaning, purposeful living, service to others. The structure of my life had imploded. I had long ago replaced the God of my youth with the god of my bottle. I was full of hatred, anger, bitterness, and resentment. I hardly knew who I was. I had heard of AA over five decades ago, but the wall of denial was so thick that I certainly didn't know I was an alcoholic.

My bottom came at a funeral, where, drunk, I insulted my dead bartender friend, along with his family and friends. Later, I lasted only 30 minutes in a psychiatrist's office and one day in an outpatient rehab program. My temporary caretaker there was a Carmelite nun who patiently listened to my psychobabble and pity-pot drivel, and then told me about AA. Finally, my younger brother, who was in the program, suggested I go to AA. "You will find answers to your questions, and a solution for your problems." So I went.

At my first meeting, which was later to become my home group, I introduced myself as an alcoholic and an ex-priest. The secretary looked me straight in the eye and said, "You are welcome. AA does not discriminate!" I began to think, This is the place.

Making changes in an old man's life proved to be a real challenge, especially radical changes. So I went to meetings twice a day, listened to what was being proclaimed, and of course took the inventory of those around me. Gradually, I distilled the basics of the AA program and its tools: Come to meetings, read the Big Book, get a sponsor, work the Steps, do service. Getting sober, walking through the horrible withdrawal, learning to listen, sharing woes without asking why, feeling the pain of ego deflation—these were the prices I had to pay. I had to experience all of them. Yet, beneath this gut-wrenching process, I had not yet fully embraced my alcoholism.

But then it happened. When I had been sober 17 months, the compulsion to drink was lifted. Rather than applaud, I asked how under the sun that had happened! I checked it out with some old-timers and then struggled with it for a month.

Up to that point, the AA program had only been in my head. Now it conquered my heart. The war was over! I had heard others talk about "surrender." Now I got down on my knees and did likewise. In so doing, I became totally convinced of the power of the AA program and Fellowship in granting me the gift of sobriety.

Each of my sponsors had provided me with specific guidance as the months progressed. Three moved out of state. Then, in the summer of 2004, I chose to study and work the Steps in a formal way with a long-time sober man who came from a background totally opposite to mine. For 16 weeks, two to three hours a week, we went through the Big Book, page by page, sometimes quickly and sometimes slowly. We discussed, we argued, and he insisted on praying. I did my Fourth, Fifth, Eighth, and Ninth Steps with him. It reminded me of taking tests during my graduate days at the university, though there is no graduation in AA.

My next sponsor was a woman who wisely insisted I get some "outside help." With her 30-some years of sobriety, she had spotted something in me that needed to be cared for by a professional.

After six months of intensive work with a therapist, I was able to rid myself of "baggage" that I had carried for 40 years. At the end, I asked what a 74-year-old alcoholic does next. The therapist simply advised me to "Pick up the pieces and mold a new life," using my AA experience as the starting point.

I reexamined everything and chose to do an "extreme makeover" on my life, even at my late stage. I laid aside all my book knowledge and former memberships in organized religion. I started with my AA experiences, where I had been given the materials and the tools for reconstructing a new way of life.

By using the Twelve Steps, I remapped my life and marked out a course of values that works for me, giving me new meaning, direction, and satisfaction in my life. Those values are my relationships to my Higher Power, to myself, and to other human beings. My new actions are surrender, sobriety, and service. In my late years, I walk this AA path one day at a time. I now enjoy the peace of mind and quiet heart that AA offers. The Promises come true.

L.H.
Reno, Nevada

ON LIVING THE AA WAY
FOR SEVEN YEARS *(Editorial)*
August 1944

Funny thing after all these years ... but it seems I haven't known too much about AA and what it really meant until just lately. And I suppose I shall go on as long as I live, and remain in AA, feeling from week to week, month to month, and maybe even year to year, that I am only just beginning to have some appreciation of what it all means, how big it is.

Sure, for over seven years now I've yapped happily about AA—what it is, how to use it, and what it could do for you—when, in reality, I had only a glimmer of its full power. But now I've seen people use it. There was the AA couple who lost three children in one week. Another couple whose only son died. Then there was the fellow who sobered up a couple of years ago and was finally able to get his wife the fur coat he had been promising for ten years ... she was killed wearing it within a week.

All of them stayed sober and I thought that was fine. They even continued to be thankful for their years of sobriety, for the way AA had helped them meet their problems. They made me feel ashamed because I didn't know how I would have reacted had these things happened to me. Then came my nephew's fatal accident and I don't think that anyone who knew my brother and me—both AAs—gave the possibility of our drinking a thought. I know at least that we didn't. And I also know that both of us had been dry long enough so that we had the boy's respect, and we are thankful for that. My brother says, "J. is where we put him when he went into the Army—in God's hands—and he's still in that care." My brother and his wife are living that way, and it is a great and merciful thing that we can feel as we do about it.

I don't mean we just say that, and then go out and play golf—we have that very human selfishness that creeps up often, of wanting him back, of feeling resentful that he was taken; but when that happens we can straighten ourselves out. We live by AA.

SPIRITUAL TOOLBOX
August 2010

One morning when my husband and I were on a road trip, we read something in *Daily Reflections* about a "spiritual kit of tools." As we drove down the highway we decided to make a list of things we would put into our spiritual toolbox. We had such fun that a few days later we stopped at a hardware store and bought the smallest toolbox we could find. We also bought a plug and receptacle so we could "plug in" to our Higher Power. These went into the box along with a Grapevine; a "God box" (a small box where I place notes to God when something troubles me); small copies of the Big Book and "Twelve and Twelve"; a small notebook and pen; and several 3 by 5 cards with reminders on them such as "Write a gratitude list from one to 10," "Rule 62," "Easy Does It" and other slogans, as well as page numbers of where to find prayers in the literature. In the tray that sits inside the top of the toolbox, I put my sponsor's phone number.

I began using this spiritual kit of tools right away and still do.

In moments of confusion I open the toolbox and invariably come across something that reminds me of how to handle a difficult situation. At other times I take out the Big Book and read a passage, or I use the tablet and pen to write something down for the God box.

Since returning home from our trip we've shared about our spiritual kit of tools at meetings and with sponsees. As a result we've heard others share what they would put into their tool kit and some sponsees have made a tool kit for themselves. Having a spiritual kit of tools in the form of a toolbox continues to be a valuable source for spiritual solutions and it's great for taking along on trips.

LYNNE C.
Bend, Oregon

IN YOUR BONES
June 2007

I remember waking up, dirty and sick, under a billboard near an apartment complex. Well-dressed men and women were getting into their cars to go to work. They stared at me with disgust and fear.

There were times I was so paranoid I'd throw myself to the ground when certain cars went by for fear that someone I'd wronged the night before might recognize me (I didn't know what I might have done).

I remember waking up in strangers' beds or in hotels I couldn't afford or at home in the afternoons on days I was supposed to be at work. I remember pouring bourbon into my coffee. I remember chasing after relatives in anger, even lust, and falling asleep, time and again, with my chin on the toilet rim.

I remember much I'm too ashamed to confess—even anonymously. There's much I don't remember, but I recollect enough to know that I don't want to go back to who I've been.

My first AA meeting was 26 years ago. I was exhausted, scared, skinny, ashamed, and aching. A group of smiling people welcomed me. Somebody asked if it was anyone's first meeting and I shakily raised my hand. In the time-honored tradition of AA, they turned their regular meeting into a First Step meeting and they told their stories.

For the next three years, I was part of a group, but not a very loyal part. My attendance was hardly religious. I took a lot and didn't give much back. I just wanted not to drink, but I was angry as all get out. I drove like a madman. I argued a lot. I even tried to throw a lawn mower through the house.

I was dry but not sober, and I didn't know the difference. Then I moved and stopped going to regular meetings.

I clung to my twenty-four hour book, and an AA uncle would check up on me now and then, but I went to only a few meetings over the next nine years. I didn't drink, but I didn't get better.

Do you need to hear it? Yelling, violence, taking it out on the kids, infidelities, lies, remorse, and loneliness, but enough success at work that I fooled people—or at least I thought I did—until two teenagers had the guts to come up to me one day and say, "It's obvious that you're angry and depressed, but it would help if you thought about what it's like to be on the other side of your face."

That got to me, and at about the same time, a friend, Bill, Twelfth-Stepped me into his AA home group. That was in 1988. Pete, the group secretary, handed me a Big Book and a "Twelve and Twelve," and said, "These are yours. We try to work the Steps."

So, every Friday night I meet with them at one or another of our homes. Every other week we study a Step, see what the Big Book or the "Twelve and Twelve" has to say about it, and then we share and reflect. The next meeting is a topic of choice, and usually the Grapevine provides the lead. This means that every year we go through the Steps twice, and believe me, there's always something newer, deeper, or fresher to learn as we get healthier.

How I've come to love those Friday nights! Something happens during the "quiet time" and the reading of "How It Works." A peace, a serenity, comes into the room. I'm in a space where my worst self is acknowledged, accepted, and welcomed with the absolute faith that I don't have to stay stuck in it. I don't fool anybody and I wouldn't want to. It feels good to shut up and listen to a lead, to learn that we're all in this together, to see sins become stories that help and heal, to watch shame turn into compassion and misery into miracles.

The guys in our group have faced some tough stuff and weathered it sober: diabetes, cancers, addictions and suicides in their families, divorces, rapes of loved ones, job losses, deaths of children.

Time and again we've talked about how the program gets into your bones, into your every thought, word, facial expression, and decision. A crisis comes and you somehow know what to do. You learn that each moment, each interaction, is an opportunity "to practice these principles in all our affairs." The Twelve Steps are medicine, reminders, practice, and review—sudden insights and inspirations that spill out into all we do.

So much that made us alcoholic lives on in us unresolved, festering, recurring in the same old patterns, expressing itself in emotional binges, intolerance, negativity, self-righteousness, self-pity, and worse. It's almost as though the program says, "Okay, you've got the poison out of your system, now let's get to work on what caused you to reach for it." That's what the Steps are for.

Only by accepting my powerlessness over alcohol did I begin to discover the powers that alcohol had obliterated: God, health, truth, love, nature, fellowship, humor, creativity, and even simple daily kindness.

Recently, I received my 26-year token. I held it toward the light, relieved that I hadn't had a drink in all that time, but humbled by the lack of quality of many of those days. But most of all, I felt gratitude for Bill W. and Dr. Bob; gratitude for those kind folks at my very first AA meeting—and at all the meetings since; for the alcoholics who have taken the time to work with other alcoholics; for my Friday night group; and gratitude for all the millions of unnamed and unknown who have worked the Twelve Steps.

JIM L.
Barrington, Illinois

I CAN SOAR *(Excerpt)*
July 2010

After many years of active alcoholism, which caused tremendous pain and suffering, not just for myself, but for those who loved me, God was able to finally get me into the rooms of Alcoholics Anonymous. It is in these rooms that I learned about fear and avoidance, about helping others, and about asking God to relieve me of my character defects. And it was in these rooms that I learned to turn my life and my will over to the care of God. I was assured that if I practiced the principles to the best of my ability, they would not only help me to stay sober a day at a time, but they also would help to change the circumstances of my life.

As I started to work on the Steps and build a sober, spiritual life, I began to feel some hope that maybe, just maybe, I could recover and even be able to do something as unimaginable as getting on an airplane without booze and without incident. In the work that was put before me, I spent considerable time asking God to remove my defects of character, particularly self-centered fear.

But the big, magic eraser I was expecting to receive that would wipe away all of these defects didn't come. I thought that I was either not completely willing or was unable to really let go. I was so accustomed to shrouding myself in fear that it was very difficult to shed that cloak. Forgetting that everything comes in God's time, the voices in my head told me to never mind, to just be happy with staying sober and not expect much else.

Then the unspeakable happened. I was confronted with a family tragedy. My future brother-in-law, who lived in Florida (no coincidences, right?), passed away very suddenly at a relatively young age.

The only way to describe this event is utter devastation. A mother lost her son, a daughter lost her father, siblings lost their brother—and I might have to fly.

Self-centeredness and fear still prevailed. Those were the defects that drove my reactions to events, big or small, like a bad reflex. Suffering from great grief and knowing of my paralyzing fear of air travel, my fiancé asked me if I'd be joining him on this sorrowful trip to Florida where his brother would be laid to rest. Contrary to what I wanted to say, God helped me utter the word yes. This time I reacted with the right reflex, but the problem with how I was going to stay true to my word now confronted me.

Thankfully, turning to alcohol did not enter my brain. Instead, it was time to really turn to God. It was time to call on the calmer voices of my friends and mentors in AA. It was time to put those Steps into action. It was truly time to let go and let God.

So onto that plane I went, without booze, without incident and without fear. With me instead was my sense of being needed to help my loved ones and the strength that I had gathered from my AA friends and most significantly God, who I knew would carry me as long as I allowed him to. This time when I stepped off the plane, I was full of gratitude and hope because I was shown, once again, that anything is possible.

Over the next two weeks of our stay, I was faced with challenges that would jolt even the toughest of souls. Each time I questioned whether I could endure anymore. But I continued to rely on the things I had: God, the Steps and the incredible Fellowship of AA. It is those things that allow me to live life as a sober woman, even in the darkest of times. I can be there for others and I can experience the miracles that are there for all of us. And I've learned that not only can I fly, I can soar!

KATHY V.
Queens, New York

ONE OF THE BIRDS
January 2009

Interviewed by Suzy P., from Upland, California, Dick C., a former drinker, gambler, and womanizer, shares his experience, strength and hope, nearly 60 years after his last drink.

SUZY P.: Dick, I really admire you. I know that you have not had a drink of alcohol since you were 34 years old and you are 93 now. You have been a really big inspiration to me and to many people at our meetings, and our Grapevine readers would really like to know your story. Can you tell us about your last drink?

DICK C.: The last drink I had was June 15, 1949. At ten o'clock in the morning a friend of mine poked me in the chest and said, "I'll tell you what I'll do. I'll buy you all the alcohol you can drink today—whatever you want—if you'll go to one Alcoholics Anonymous meeting with me tonight." He was a person who had money and was willing to spend it, and I said, "Sure." I drank that day and we went to the meeting that night. I recognized three people there and thought, What the hell's going on here with these nuts that quit drinking? When the meeting was over, I went to sleep on some chairs in the back of the room. Three days later, I had the DTs. I yelled and screamed, I refused a drink, I refused a doctor, but those people from the meeting kept on talking to me. To make a long story short, it's just one day at a time, and I've been able to stay sober from that day to this.

S.: How often do you attend meetings?

D.: Well, years ago these towns around Pomona, Upland, and Ontario had only one meeting per week, so we went in caravans. Four or five cars would get together, and we'd go to different places. We even went where they weren't having a meeting at the time, and we'd get enough people together and start our own. Today, I average at least a meeting a day.

S.: What do you like about meetings?

D.: You know the old saying "birds of a feather flock together"? Well, after a while, if you're going to meetings you realize that you're one of the birds! And you're flocking with a bunch of other birds that you recognize—you recognize the way they talk and so forth, and you realize that's where you belong. You see, drinking and gambling and women were my life beforehand; now Alcoholics Anonymous and associating with people like myself is what keeps me going.

S.: How do you think AA will change in the future?

D.: I don't think AA per se will change in the future. I've noticed in the past few years that a number of drug addicts are coming in lately and after meeting them and talking with them I have discovered that they seem to find more peace of mind in AA meetings than they do in other fellowships. But, we should be clear in telling them that this is Alcoholics Anonymous. Ultimately, if we're not clear about this up front, a time will come when you may not recognize the meeting as being strictly an Alcoholics Anonymous meeting.

A lot of us are convinced that alcohol is not the problem—we're the problem. Alcohol can sit in the bottle for 100 years if you just leave it alone. It's we alcoholics who have an allergy of the body and an obsession of the mind that makes us unable to handle it. In general, a social drinker can say, "Let's go have a drink," and a lot of times that's what they do, go have a drink. But, as an alcoholic, we go have a drunk; we drink beyond our capacity to handle it.

S.: Did you get to meet Bill W.?

D.: I never shook Bill W.'s hand, but I've been in his presence twice at conventions—I'd say five or six feet away. Also, I got to see Dr. Bob once. They were fine-looking men, and you just felt good to be in their presence. I've met plenty of wonderful people in Alcoholics Anonymous, but those two were impressive.

S.: Can you imagine your life without AA?

D.: No, because this is how I got sober, through applying the teachings of AA to my own life. I think I have a better chance of going without certain foods or water or whatever, but Alcoholics Anonymous, after a while it just becomes a part of you. It goes back to that old saying I mentioned earlier about birds of a feather flocking together. That's just the way it is. People come into AA, and they think, Well, that doesn't work for me. But that's because they're not working it, not because it doesn't work. It will work.

S.: Do you know anybody who has been sober as long as you?

D.: No, I am looking for someone who's been sober longer so I can get him to be my sponsor. Anyway, so far I haven't found anyone. I'm sure there are some that are around, maybe in a rest home, or whatever. They're just not around here. Nevertheless, it's sure good to be sober today.

SUZY P.
Upland, California

OIL AND WATER *(from Dear Grapevine)*
March 2007

My friend, Norma, came to AA at the age of 62. She has been sober for 24 years. Norma and I fit the phrase: "We are people who normally would not mix." We are from different generations and backgrounds. Yet, we enjoy each other's company at AA meetings and other outside activities.

In sobriety, Norma has faced many physical infirmities, including Parkinson's Disease, a heart condition, and macular degeneration. But as her physical condition deteriorated, Norma's spirituality seemed to increase. She faced each setback with grace and dignity, ever grateful for the simple things in life and appreciative of what she perceives as God's continuous blessings.

When I hear complaints about things that seem trivial, I think of the courage she exhibits. Now confined mainly to home, Norma is an example of grace under pressure. There are many ways to share experience, strength, and hope in our program. Norma shares hers by example.

JOANNE M.
East Amherst, New York

RECOVERY ISLAND *(from Dear Grapevine)*
January 2007

I am seven months and two days sober as I write this letter from Alaska. Before coming here to work, I was afraid I wouldn't be able to attend meetings and stay sober. So my friend Rick L. walked me around the grounds of the club where we hold our meetings in Phoenix, Arizona. Each time we got to a different spot, he asked me, "Do you think God is with you?"

"Yes," I replied.

He assured me that when I traveled to Alaska, God would be there with me, too.

Once here, I attended the twenty-fourth annual Ketchikan AA Roundup. I even got a temporary sponsor. Although I am currently isolated from meetings, I know that as long as I keep asking God for help, reading the Grapevine, listening to AA tapes, and calling my sponsors, God will not let me down.

I am surrounded by alcoholism: 75 percent of the crew drink. So, as I need to, I retreat back to the confines of my bunk. I pray, read, and use the tools in my recovery toolbox. I do the things I need to do to stay sober.

My prayer today is to continue to put God first, as he will do for me what I've never been able to do for myself.

DOUGLAS R.
Ketchikan, Alaska

THE TWELVE STEPS

1. We admitted we were powerless over alcohol—that our lives had become unmanageable.
2. Came to believe that a Power greater than ourselves could restore us to sanity.
3. Made a decision to turn our will and our lives over to the care of God *as we understood Him*.
4. Made a searching and fearless moral inventory of ourselves.
5. Admitted to God, to ourselves, and to another human being the exact nature of our wrongs.
6. Were entirely ready to have God remove all these defects of character.
7. Humbly asked Him to remove our shortcomings.
8. Made a list of all persons we had harmed, and became willing to make amends to them all.
9. Made direct amends to such people wherever possible, except when to do so would injure them or others.
10. Continued to take personal inventory and when we were wrong promptly admitted it.
11. Sought through prayer and meditation to improve our conscious contact with God *as we understood Him*, praying only for knowledge of His will for us and the power to carry that out.
12. Having had a spiritual awakening as the result of these steps, we tried to carry this message to alcoholics, and to practice these principles in all our affairs.

THE TWELVE TRADITIONS

1. Our common welfare should come first; personal recovery depends upon A.A. unity.
2. For our group purpose there is but one ultimate authority—a loving God as He may express Himself in our group conscience. Our leaders are but trusted servants; they do not govern.
3. The only requirement for A.A. membership is a desire to stop drinking.
4. Each group should be autonomous except in matters affecting other groups or A.A. as a whole.
5. Each group has but one primary purpose—to carry its message to the alcoholic who still suffers.
6. An A.A. group ought never endorse, finance or lend the A.A. name to any related facility or outside enterprise, lest problems of money, property and prestige divert us from our primary purpose.
7. Every A.A. group ought to be fully self-supporting, declining outside contributions.
8. Alcoholics Anonymous should remain forever nonprofessional, but our service centers may employ special workers.
9. A.A., as such, ought never be organized; but we may create service boards or committees directly responsible to those they serve.
10. Alcoholics Anonymous has no opinion on outside issues; hence the A.A. name ought never be drawn into public controversy.
11. Our public relations policy is based on attraction rather than promotion; we need always maintain personal anonymity at the level of press, radio and films.
12. Anonymity is the spiritual foundation of all our traditions, ever reminding us to place principles before personalities.

Alcoholics Anonymous

AA's program of recovery is fully set forth in its basic text, *Alcoholics Anonymous* (commonly known as the Big Book), now in its Fourth Edition, as well as in *Twelve Steps and Twelve Traditions*, *Living Sober*, and other books. Information on AA can also be found on AA's website at www.aa.org, or by writing to: Alcoholics Anonymous, Box 459, Grand Central Station, New York, NY 10163. For local resources, check your local telephone directory under "Alcoholics Anonymous." Four pamphlets, "This is A.A.," "Is A.A. For You?," "44 Questions," and "A Newcomer Asks" are also available from AA.

AA Grapevine

AA Grapevine is AA's international monthly journal, published continuously since its first issue in June 1944. The AA pamphlet on AA Grapevine describes its scope and purpose this way: "As an integral part of Alcoholics Anonymous for more than sixty years, Grapevine publishes articles that reflect the full diversity of experience and thought found within the AA fellowship. No one viewpoint or philosophy dominates its pages, and in determining content, the editorial staff relies on the principles of the Twelve Traditions." AA Grapevine also publishes La Viña, AA's Spanish-language print magazine, which serves the Hispanic AA community.

In addition to magazines, AA Grapevine, Inc. also produces books, eBooks, audiobooks, and other items. It also offers a Grapevine Online subscription, which includes: five new stories weekly, AudioGrapevine (the audio version of the magazine), Grapevine Story Archive (the entire collection of Grapevine articles), and the current issue of Grapevine and La Viña in HTML format. A Story Archive subscription is also available individually. For more information on AA Grapevine, or to subscribe to any of these, please visit the magazine's website at WWW.AAGRAPEVINE.ORG or write to:

AA Grapevine, Inc.
475 Riverside Drive
New York, NY 10115